*Historical Association*

Women
in an Industrializing Society:
England 1750–1880

## Historical Association Studies

*General Editors: M. E. Chamberlain and James Shields*

China in the Twentieth Century
*Paul Bailey*

The Agricultural Revolution
*J. V. Beckett*

Class, Party and the Political System in
Britain 1867–1914
*John Belchem*

The Ancien Régime
*Peter Campbell*

Decolonization
The Fall of the European Empires
*M. E. Chamberlain*

Gandhi
*Anthony Copley*

The Counter-Reformation
*N. S. Davidson*

British Radicalism and the French
Revolution 1789–1815
*H. T. Dickinson*

From Luddism to the First Reform Bill
Reform in England 1810–1832
*J. R. Dinwiddy*

Radicalism in the English Revolution
1640–1660
*F. D. Dow*

Revolution and Counter-Revolution in
France 1815–1852
*William Fortescue*

The New Monarchy
England, 1471–1534
*Anthony Goodman*

The French Reformation
*Mark Greengrass*

Politics in the Reign of Charles II
*K. H. D. Haley*

Occupied France
Collaboration and Resistance 1940–1944
*H. R. Kedward*

Secrecy in Britain
*Clive Ponting*

Women in an Industrializing Society:
England 1750–1880
*Jane Rendall*

Appeasement
*Keith Robbins*

Franklin D. Roosevelt
*Michael Simpson*

Britain's Decline
Problems and Perspectives
*Alan Sked*

The Cold War 1945–1965
*Joseph Smith*

Bismarck
*Bruce Waller*

The Russian Revolution 1917–1921
*Beryl Williams*

The Historical Association, founded in 1906, brings together people who share an interest in, and love for, the past. It aims to further the study and teaching of history at all levels: teacher and student, amateur and professional. This is one of over 100 publications available at preferential rates to members. Membership also includes journals at generous discounts and gives access to courses, conferences, tours and regional and local activities. Full details are available from The Secretary, The Historical Association, 59a Kennington Park Road, London SE11 4JH, telephone: 071-735 3901.

# Women
# in an Industrializing
# Society: England
# 1750–1880

*Jane Rendall*

BLACKWELL
*Oxford UK & Cambridge USA*

Copyright © Jane Rendall 1990

First published 1990
First published in USA 1991
Reprinted 1993, 1994

Blackwell Publishers
108 Cowley Road, Oxford, OX4 1JF, UK

238 Main Street
Cambridge, Massachusetts 02142, USA

*British Library Cataloguing in Publication Data*

A CIP catalogue record for this book is available from the British Library.

*Library of Congress Cataloging in Publication Data*

Rendall, Jane, 1945–
    Women and industrialization in England, 1750–1880/Jane Rendall.
        p.   cm. — (Historical Association studies)
    Includes bibliographical references.
    ISBN 0–631–15303–9
        1. Women—Employment—England—History.   2. Home economics—
    England—History.   3. England—Industries—History.   4. Work and family—
    England—History.   5. Middle classes—England—History.
    I. Title.   II. Series.
    HD7024.R46 1991
    331.4′0941′09034—dc20                                                    90–261
                                                                              CIP

Typeset in 11 on 13 pt Ehrhardt
by Setrite Typesetters Ltd, Hong Kong
Printed and bound in Great Britain by Hartnolls Limited, Bodmin, Cornwall

This book is printed on acid-free paper.

# Contents

# *Acknowledgements*

I should like to thank the Historical Association's editors and readers and Jenny Tyler for their comments and suggestions. I should also like to thank Angela John for kind permission to reprint the table on p. 56.

# Introduction

There are a number of familiar and appealing images which tend to dominate any discussion about Victorian women: the 'angel in the house', the 'factory girl', the domestic servant. These images offer a series of simple interpretations of women's lives in the changing society of the nineteenth century. Yet our 'Victorian' views of nineteenth-century women seem to be based on the artificially constructed dates of a reign. We need to look at a longer and more gradual pattern of changes affecting the relations between women and men in a developing industrial society. Historians have recently suggested that the pattern we see should be a far more complex one, drawing in the profound differences that existed between different classes in society and between different regions of England. Our popular images may contain some aspects of this more complex picture, but may also confuse more than they help.

There is, first, the ideal of the 'angel in the house', the 'leisured lady'. These two terms are not of course identical, though they are often used as if they were. Both, however, emerged from the assumption of an absolute separation between the inner sanctum of the home and the outer masculine world of business, politics and public affairs in the nineteenth century. Such a separation can be contrasted with the involvement of the urban woman of the pre-industrial past in her husband's business or the family enterprise. The new, confined domestic sphere could imply a life of idleness and frivolity for the middle-class woman with such good fortune. But more often, the 'leisure' purchased through the employment of a large household of servants was to be put to uplifting uses. The term 'angel in the house' comes from a poem by Coventry Patmore written in 1854 at the height of mid-Victorian sentimentality. This suggests a life withdrawn from the mundane realities of the everyday world, a life which implied confinement to a domestic sphere. The spiritual rather than the practical aspects of such domesticity are emphasized when describing such a Victorian woman. The 'angel' was required to be pure, asexual, submissive yet morally superior and capable of preserving within the home those moral values which might be in danger outside it.

This ideal had been for many years fostered by those, both men and women, who wrote the advice manuals or prescriptive literature addressed to women. For instance, Hannah More in the 1790s, in the early years of the evangelical revival in the Anglican Church, had called for women to focus their influence within the domestic sphere:

> A woman sees the world, as it were, from a little elevation in her own garden, whence she makes an exact survey of home scenes, but takes not in that wider range of distant prospects which he, who stands on a loftier eminence, commands. (1818, p. 29)

Evangelical writers of different denominations continued to spread such ideas for the next fifty years or more. Mrs Sarah Ellis wrote a whole series of works, entitled *The Women of England* (1839), *The Daughters of England* (1842), *The Wives of England* (1843) and *The Mothers of England* (1843). Hannah More and many later writers conceived that once established the superior influence of women should be spread far beyond the domestic hearth, uplifting the moral condition of society more generally by example, by the education of children and through philanthropic good works. Another writer, Sarah Lewis, in *Woman's Mission* (1839) wrote of a missionary role for women. There was nothing new in such ideas at the beginning of Queen Victoria's reign in 1837. Indeed they were a part of the assumptions and the language of middle-class men and women, and strongly influenced their reactions to working-class women's lives.

Yet it is too easy to take such prescriptive works as indicating the realities for middle-class women. Clearly many read such works and heard such messages in their churches and chapels. Yet 'leisure' required a substantial income, and a number of servants. Only the wealthier sections of the middle classes could afford to live in that way. Most middle-class women retained the daily responsibilities of running a household — and their lives were not necessarily 'leisured'. As middle-class homes consumed and become the showplaces for the new products of an industrializing economy — stoves, carpets, curtains, china — the tasks of shopping for, cleaning and maintaining the home became more rather than less complex. Not all middle-class women lived in households as separate from the public world as is implied by the ideal suggested. Family lives and business affairs might be closely interwoven for much of this period. The close connections between the industrializing economy of the nineteenth century and the private domestic worlds of the middle classes have to be explored carefully. Only then can we fully understand the meaning of that separation of the spheres of women and men in the middle classes of Victorian society — a separation which had profound consequences for women and men of all classes.

The second image which tends to dominate thinking about women in nineteenth-century England is that of the 'factory girl' — usually implying a worker in one of the Lancashire cotton mills. It is this figure which seems to symbolize the dramatic changes which industrialization brought working-class women. In the pre-industrial economy, it is sometimes argued, single and married women alike worked within their families, taking on a range of tasks, especially those connected with the production of wool, cotton and silk. The factory system ended that flexible, familiar pattern of work, and in separating the workplace from the home subjected women as

3

well as men to new forms of labour. Such labour required women and girls to work very long hours, poorly paid, in often appalling conditions, and by separating them not only from their home but from their family responsibilities fragmented family life. The powerful images conveyed by mid-nineteenth-century novelists like Elizabeth Gaskell reflected the social concerns of reformers and parliamentarians, voiced above all in the great parliamentary enquiries of the 1830s and 1840s. They were concerned at the moral dangers existing for women and girls working outside the home, at the absence of domestic care and domestic training for families this entailed and at the extent to which the authority of fathers might be undermined. Those who have looked at these issues from a twentieth-century viewpoint, however, have tended to ask whether our sources on these questions do not themselves reflect a particular bias: the bias of a middle class which saw the working-class family through its own spectacles, and stressed the dramatic and catastrophic impact of industrialization.

The factory and the factory girls were symbols of the new economic order, and as symbols they dominated debate. Yet even in the 1840s women working in factories were a minority. Other forms of production, some of which retained the old family form of manufacture, were still of great importance. Women's involvement in manufacturing *work* was not a product of the early nineteenth century. Of course working-class women had always worked in early modern England, though they normally received significantly lower wages than men. And the eighteenth century had seen a steady expansion of women's involvement in domestic manufacture, both in their homes and in small workshops. Technological development did gradually change that work; but only in a few regions and industries was that change dramatic. The overlap between home and work continued to be one theme of women's work, as the old domestic manufacture of the countryside, still flourishing in the early nineteenth century, gave way to the 'sweated trades' of the great urban centres. In an expanding economy, entrepreneurs looked for the most profitable way to organize their businesses, whether through the use of new

4

technology or by employing the cheapest labour. Women and girls − already recognized as cheaper labour − might be most profitably employed in cottage, workshop or factory. Industrialization did not necessarily mean a dramatic or immediate shift to factory production.

There are other kinds of questions which historians now put about women's involvement in industrial change which do not draw their inspiration from the concerns of the mid-nineteenth-century reformer. These are questions relevant not only to the cotton mills, but to the hosiery industries of the East Midlands, the metal workshops of Birmingham and the potteries in the Black Country. Technological change brought with it a clearer division of labour between women and men: such a division had always existed within the family, though probably there was a degree of flexibility and interchangeability. Now the line between 'men's work' and 'women's work' was to be much more sharply drawn, in the home, the workshop and the factory. Skilled work was a masculine domain: women's work was unskilled or semi-skilled, paid at much lower rates. How − and on what basis − were these distinctions between the work of men and women, of girls and boys and of girls and women drawn? How far did a view of women as wives and daughters, with family responsibilities and at the same time subject to the authority of husbands and fathers within the family, influence their place within the world of work?

The third familiar image is that of the Victorian domestic servant, living in the world 'below stairs' serving the leisured middle classes, and in the aristocracy's great town and country houses. Victorian household manuals like Mrs Beeton's *Book of Household Management* (1861) tell us of the expectations of such servants' work. Domestic servants, according to the census figures of the second half of the nineteenth century, were the largest single group of women workers. Yet the majority of servants did not work in aristocratic or wealthy households or even in households where there were other servants. Mainly they worked as general servants in the households of tradesmen, shopkeepers or artisans, or in the new suburbs. So they were likely to do the hard domestic work of the small household without companionship and for little reward.

There are more problems for any student of domestic service. Our understanding of it tends to be drawn primarily from the census figures, yet these figures are unreliable: contemporaries did not always distinguish between servants and family members. And the world of domestic labour has been neglected and undervalued by historians. We need more studies of the kind of work performed by servants, which we cannot always clearly grasp if we rely on twentieth-century concepts of domesticity.

This review of some familiar figures has already suggested new questions about the changes in women's lives in the nineteenth century. Social and economic historians have for some years come to suggest a rather different picture of the process of industrialization, seeing it as less dramatic, more gradual and more diverse than the term 'industrial revolution' might imply. Women were a part of, influenced by and influencing, that process. That is why the period discussed here is a different, and longer, one from that addressed by Ivy Pinchbeck in her classic work, *Women Workers and the Industrial Revolution* (1930). In that work Pinchbeck assumed that dramatic changes in women's lives were due to industrialization. The fundamental question she asked was this: 'was industrialization a good thing for women?' This is still a matter for debate among historians. In the past, much attention was paid to the 'factory girl' and to the 'opportunities' offered by factory production and new technologies for women's employment. Ivy Pinchbeck argued:

> In the case of the single working woman, the most striking effect of the industrial revolution was her distinct gain in social and economic independence. In industries in which a family wage prevailed, women scarcely knew the extent of, or had any opportunity of handling, their own earnings, and among women who earned an individual wage, few earned sufficient to give them any real sense of independence. Under the new regime every woman received her own earnings as a matter of course. (1981, p. 313)

To Pinchbeck, industrialization brought benefits both to the married woman – who for the first time, she suggested, was expected to give her sole attention to the care of home and children – and to the single woman, who experienced a new sense of economic independence.

Pinchbeck's work is still of great importance, and for the moment remains the major survey of the impact of industrialization on women workers in Britain. Most modern historians would see her interpretation, however, as unduly optimistic. They would suggest that she paid too much attention here to the gains of the 'factory girl', too little to the majority of working women, and also too little to the continuing work of married women; even for the 'factory girl' the benefits may seem exaggerated for the period under discussion. A longer perspective than that taken by Pinchbeck and one which is not based on assumptions of an industrial 'revolution' can be more useful in determining what really happened to women. So, for instance, historical work is gradually revising our understanding of the ways in which women were actively involved in eighteenth-century industry and agriculture. We can trace the transition from such involvement to the apparently sharper divisions between the worlds of women and men that seem to mark the mid to late Victorian period. We shall find more continuities than earlier historians such as Pinchbeck did; we may also find new ways of looking at the importance of these changes brought about by industrial development, most obviously and most critically the separation of the home from the workplace.

The study of women's history has expanded greatly since Pinchbeck wrote, especially over the last ten to fifteen years. It has prompted some new ways of looking at women's lives, moving away from older stereotypes, increasing our knowledge of continuities as well as changes. The major landmarks of our history – the Renaissance, the Reformation, the industrial revolution – have not necessarily affected women in the same way as men. There are four questions which can be picked out for our discussion of the impact of industrialization on women.

First, what was the *meaning* of the word 'work' to nineteenth-century women (and men)? In the censuses of the early nineteenth century it is never clear whether it is the work of

7

households or of individuals which is being counted. Even later, the census figures may often confuse when paid and unpaid domestic work can be identified: women may not have thought of themselves as workers if, for instance, they took in laundry or sewing, or did a little hawking, selling goods in the streets. The shift from the idea of work as the occupation of a family to work as the waged labour of an individual presents us with particular problems in relation to women – did they see themselves as individual waged workers, or in relation to a family's earning power?

Second, there is the interaction between the family lives of women and their working lives. The study of paid employment in the nineteenth century cannot be separated from the study of the family, in both the middle classes and the working classes. The marriage of a middle-class young woman might be of great importance to the family business. Working-class women and men would find the nature of their work influenced how long they waited to get married, how many children they had and whether a married woman was likely to work for money outside the home. It is important also to look at the structure of authority within the family. Both legally and by custom, husbands and fathers exerted very great powers to exact obedience from wives and daughters: how far were those powers extended to the world of paid employment outside the home?

Third, any study of women's lives has to reinstate the importance of all forms of domestic labour, paid and unpaid, in middle-class and working-class households. Manufacture carried on within the home remained of importance throughout most of this period. Changing patterns of housing, of sanitation and of domestic technology meant new conditions of labour, of shopping, cooking and washing. Depending on a person's income level, new industrial products brought aspirations towards forms of domesticity. New demands on mothers in the task of childcare could be made by the medical profession and by reformers.

Finally, the nineteenth century was a period which saw sharpening divisions between the worlds of women and of men, though these divisions did not always take the same forms. In the middle classes, the strength of the ideal of separate spheres — of different domestic and public worlds — was clear, though it obscured the real interconnections of those worlds. For working-class women and men, economic changes brought different forms of separation — in the kind of work done within the factories and workshops, and ultimately in the separation of home and work. These processes brought new definitions of the appropriate division of labour for men and women. It is important to note that these new definitions might themselves vary and were by no means uniform throughout the country. They might be described as 'natural', yet arose out of particular sets of economic and social assumptions. Here is an example of one such differing set of views, in an exchange between Lord Manners, a Leicestershire MP serving on the 1854 select committee on hosiery manufacture, and Richard Muggeridge, who had studied and come to share the views of local Leicestershire framework knitters:

> Lord Manners:   Speaking generally from your experience, and with the knowledge you possess of the labouring classes, are you of the opinion that it is a beneficial thing, with a view to the management of a family and the domestic economy of a cottage, that the female head of that family should be employed ... in manufacture?
>
> Richard Muggeridge:   No, certainly not. I do think that the mother of a family ought always to find enough to do without being employed at frame work. There are many things which she might do to assist the family, such, for instance, as seaming, which is quite a woman's work. (Quoted in Osterud, 1986, p. 53)

Here the questioner, Lord Manners, assuming that domestic economy and paid work were incompatible, expected a rather different answer from the one he received. Male Leicestershire framework knitters *did* see it as the married woman's responsibility to do paid work — as long as it was done within the

9

household. In Leicester, the division of labour between men and women in the hosiery industry had become established: framework knitting had moved into workshops by mid-century but seaming remained a task normally performed at home in the 1850s. Unfortunately we have very little evidence of the views of working-class women themselves.

Here we shall look not so much at the benefits and disadvantages of industrialization for women's lives but at the new light which has been thrown on the subject through the advances in women's history and social history over the last ten to fifteen years. The new perspectives have been prompted by a desire to understand the historical forces which shaped women's lives, and especially the interaction between economic changes and the world of the family. It is an issue of considerable importance not merely to the understanding of nineteenth-century England. A grasp of the shape of the changes of the nineteenth century may lead to a far better knowledge of the sexual division of labour of late-twentieth-century England. And our awareness of how industrial growth may affect the relationship between women and men may be relevant to the study of other industrializing societies, both of the past and of the present.

# 1

## Women's Paid Employment 1750–1830

When Ivy Pinchbeck wrote her classic study, historians' views of the economy of this period were dominated by two major concepts: the 'agricultural revolution' and the 'industrial revolution'. Today both have been subject to major revisions. The old view suggested, first, that the second half of the eighteenth century was a period which saw an 'agrarian revolution' which would sweep away older practices of farming mainly for subsistence and local markets, replacing them by a new commercial system dependent on the large farm and the landless labourer. But new work by economic and agricultural historians has transformed this picture: we now see agricultural growth and a market-oriented countryside as of far greater importance from at least the late seventeenth century onwards, if not earlier. It was the agricultural innovations of the late seventeenth and early eighteenth centuries which fostered the large-scale farms, dependent on capital investment, of the arable corn-growing areas of southern and eastern England. Though the second half of the century was a major period for parliamentary enclosures, these were more important for areas of mixed farming like the Midlands. New work has emphasized the importance of regional differences in agriculture, and especially the contrast between the capitalized, corn-growing south and east and the pastoral regions of the north and west.

Similarly, the eighteenth century as a whole saw the expansion of manufactures throughout the countryside, mainly on a domestic basis. There was clear growth in real output from most British industries from the 1740s, perhaps earlier. The most dramatic changes were in the textile industries — cotton, wool and silk — but also in other forms of industry. Most of those who worked in their homes or in small workshops lived in the countryside, and worked for merchants who put out to them work in spinning, knitting or weaving. Increasingly they found the conditions under which they lived and worked were dependent on the prices paid in international markets. Industrial employment might be a useful means of supplementing the family economy, or it might provide employment for the whole family: for men, women, children and indeed for whole villages. But above all, the expansion of these industries meant a steady growth in the labour of women and children. Their labour was cheap. Sometimes it would be most profitable to employ new technology, and to employ workers in large factories. But just as often, employers found it most advantageous to maintain and expand the domestic basis of production. Or they might use small workshops, or divide the work that had to be done between men's work in workshops, and women's work in household manufacture.

However, when we look for reliable information from this period about the productive work that women did, sources are scarce. The surveys on which historians base their estimates of occupational patterns in the eighteenth century are based on the occupations of households. So too are the censuses, which began in 1801 and until 1841 recorded the occupations of households rather than individuals. It was taken for granted that husband, wife and children all contributed to the occupation of each household, though both those who did the counting and those householders who sent in returns were rather confused about this: as was recorded in the 1831 census report:

In some cases a householder seemed to understand that the females of his family, his children and servants ought to be classed with himself, in some cases he returned them in the negative class, as being neither agricultural nor commercial; in some cases he omitted them entirely. (Quoted in Hakim, 1980, p. 554)

So, we have no reliable quantitative estimates of the work done by women (or men) in this critical period. There were, however, a number of important qualitative surveys of particular industries and regions which can be drawn upon, although the major parliamentary surveys of the work of women and children began only in the 1830s. Recently economic historians have started to use other kinds of records for precisely this purpose. Poor Law records, for instance, may be used to establish the patterns of employment of women as agricultural labourers, and urban records tell us something of the entry of women into apprenticeships. But the task of reconstructing a reliable picture is a challenging one; much research remains to be done.

WOMEN IN THE COUNTRYSIDE

It is difficult to separate the different kinds of paid work in agriculture and in domestic industry which women in the countryside were likely to undertake. At different times of the year married women would be likely to do whatever kind of work offered most help to the family economy. However, the economic changes of this period did have overall consequences for women's work. The move was towards larger-scale enterprises in both agriculture and industry: since capital had to produce the most profitable returns, this could mean greater specialization in production, and also perhaps a greater and more clearly defined division of labour between women and men.

Ivy Pinchbeck's study of women's agricultural work — so detailed and so meticulous in its research that it has remained unchallenged as a major source — was based on an assumption of major changes taking place in the late eighteenth century. Pinchbeck traced the effect which the shift from smaller to

13

larger, more commercially oriented farms had on the wife of a tentant farmer, who was more likely to withdraw from being actively involved in managing the farm. She noted the impact which enclosures were likely to have on the poorer farmer's or cottager's wife who might formerly have kept a small amount of land and animals, with common rights. And she noted the decline in the numbers of farm servants, both women and men, who had lived in as servants on farms. These servants were being replaced by a smaller, male workforce, living out, and by seasonal and casual labourers. All these themes remain of importance, though they were probably taking place over a longer timescale than Pinchbeck suggested. The overall direction of change was that of the declining role of women in agricultural work, already apparent, though not very clearly, by the 1830s.

Research suggests to us some new aspects of a revised picture. In the south and east of Britain much agricultural land had already been enclosed by the mid-eighteenth century; in these areas, especially, changes in agricultural practice were able to increase the extent of arable farming and to make it far more efficient and productive. Studies of male and female unemployment in these areas through the Poor Law records have suggested that the distribution of work on the land between men and women in these areas was already shifting by the mid-eighteenth century. Until then the demand for male and female workers had been similar, and constant throughout the year. But demands for greater efficiency brought the adoption of a new technology, if a primitive one. On the larger farms the old sickle, wielded by both men and women at harvest time, was giving way to the much heavier and more difficult to use scythe. There was a greater degree of specialization in tasks to be performed. Men were more likely to be employed all the year round, because of their utility at harvest time. Women were more likely to be employed as casual labour at certain times of the year, especially in spring for weeding and sowing, and their wages fell.

In other areas of the country there were different patterns of agricultural specialization: in the north and west and in some parts of the Midlands, livestock and dairy farming expanded. Here the demand for women's work if anything increased, and it has been suggested that their real wages increased.

These shifts were linked to other changes in the structure of the agricultural workforce. As Pinchbeck suggested, from the 1820s onwards there was much contemporary discussion of a decline in farm service, especially in the southeast. Farm service meant the hiring of women and men as servants at an annual hiring fair, for an agreed sum; they lived in with full board on the farm. Women farm servants might be required to do a range of tasks, including field work, probably with no very clear distinction between what might be done in or outside the farmhouse. Some women might be hired for more specialist work, especially within the dairy, which was seen very much as a woman's task. Service, in this context, meant work done by a young woman before marriage: working in another household, but not confined to household work, and contributing to most farm work as needed.

In the south and east there was clearly a greater tendency to employ labourers living in their own cottages, or casual workers. Sometimes farmers' wives were blamed for this change. Living on larger, more prosperous farms, they were accused of having undue aspirations towards gentility, of wanting to be like ladies – buying pianos for their parlours and sending their daughters to boarding schools, no longer boarding and living with their labourers. It was, however, also true that farmers were more reluctant to have living-in servants, since if they were resident they might qualify for poor relief, adding to the burden on ratepayers. However, farm service remained a very important area of work for unmarried women on the smaller, pastoral farms of the north and west of the country throughout this period. These were areas of generally smaller farms and especially of pastoral and dairy farming, in which women were still acknowledged to have a particular role. There was also, especially in the north, much more competition from industrial employment for men's labour.

The overall direction of these changes was to separate the occupations of servant and farm labourer. The married, men and women, were as likely to be employed as labourers as the unmarried. The older meaning of service − a period of employment in another household before one's own marriage, a stage in the life-cycle as much as an occupation − was to survive mainly in the continuing employment of young country-women as domestic servants rather than as farm servants.

But casual employment for married and unmarried women on the land did remain of some importance, at least into the first half of the nineteenth century. Enclosures of new land had significant social effects which, since Pinchbeck wrote, have been much debated. The most recent work, that of Keith Snell, has suggested that the pattern of enclosures in the second half of the eighteenth century did much to consolidate the trend towards sexual specialization in agricultural work. Married women had for centuries worked when they were required and when they needed to on the land; at the same time, as a part of a flexible family economy, they had worked for themselves on small plots of land, on cottage gardens, tending their livestock on the common lands, as well as spinning. Now they no longer had that resource, but were dependent on what casual paid work was offered to them. And in areas where male unemployment was high, that meant competition with male workers. In arable areas, then, women could expect only casual employment in the spring and early summer − weeding, sowing, stone picking, haymaking and sometimes the harvesting of root crops. At times of a shortage of male labour, as in the Napoleonic Wars, the demand for their services might temporarily increase, but it would always be dependent on local crops and the availability of male labourers.

Even by the late eighteenth century the contrast between the rural economies of northern and southern England was clear, and by the mid-nineteenth century it was commonplace. In the north and west a pastoral agriculture and the presence of alternative industrial employment helped to keep up the demand for, and the wages of, women workers on the land. But agricultural efficiency in arable production had brought with it an impoverished labour force in the south. Young women in these areas had little choice but to leave their parental homes to seek work not on the land but in domestic service or manufacture. Married women struggled to help maintain their families, facing dire poverty and the threat of the workhouse. A more specialized agricultural economy had brought with it striking divisions in levels of prosperity, as well as a much clearer division of labour between women and men.

By the beginning of the Victorian period, new attitudes to women's work on the land were apparent. In the Royal Commission of 1843, witnesses commented on the absence of women workers; one said

> I remember formerly when girls turned out regularly with the boys to plough etc., and were up to the knees in dirt, and in the middle of winter in all kinds of employment. Now you never see a girl about in the fields. (Quoted in Pinchbeck, 1981, p. 109)

Again we have little evidence for the views of women working on the land themselves, though the voice of one or two can be heard through evidence given to the parliamentary commissioners, like that of the forty-eight-year-old Jane Long:

> I never felt the work hurt me, not when a girl more than since I have been grown up. I often come home too tired to do anything but always with a good appetite. I was always better when working out in the fields than when I was staying at home. (Report of the Commissioners on the Employment of Women and Children in Agriculture, 1843, XII, pp. 70–1)

By the middle of the nineteenth century, Victorians were expressing clear disapproval of such outdoor activity by women of all ages. But it is evident that it was not such disapproval which brought about the decline of women agricultural workers, but more fundamental economic shifts, begun a century earlier.

The New Poor Law of 1834, designed for the conditions of

17

the rural south, was also to affect women's work on the land. In removing outdoor relief to able-bodied men, it increased the pressures on married women to find some kind of paid employment locally, at whatever minimal rates of pay. In East Anglia, the reluctance of farmers and landowners to employ men who might become entitled to poor relief led to the development of 'gangs' of women and children moving around the country under a gang-master. This met the need for casual labour at certain times of the year, without involving farmers in any extra commitment to permanently employed workers.

But women's work in the countryside was never confined to agricultural work on the land. Women and girls were employed in various kinds of rural industry across the country throughout the eighteenth century. One such area of employment, which responded to new economic developments, was of course coal-mining, which like agricultural work required heavy physical labour of women, and was undertaken largely within the family economy. In the eighteenth century women were employed extensively as part of a family group, hired and paid by a male member. They worked mainly as drawers, pulling sledges or tubs full of coal along the pit floor. However, by the late eighteenth and early nineteenth century this pattern was declining, though we have little information on the exact timing of this decline. Women no longer worked in the Northumberland and Durham coalfields after 1780, nor in those of the Midlands. They were still employed in the 1840s in Yorkshire and Lancashire, in South Wales and, most of all, in eastern Scotland, but such work may have been at its height in the eighteenth century. After that the introduction of horses and a few wheeled vehicles on iron rails saw boys taking the drawing jobs, possibly because this was seen as part of a miner's apprenticeship, possibly because it appeared more dangerous.

Recent estimates of occupational patterns in eighteenth-century England suggest that by the end of the century employment in different forms of industry was as important as employment in agriculture: England was already a manufacturing nation. One estimate suggests that employment in textiles more than tripled during the second half of the

18

eighteenth century (Lindert, 1980). This expansion meant the extensive employment of women and children in all forms of the textile industry in the countryside – cotton, wool, linen and silk. Domestic industry or outwork was not, however, confined to the textile industry.

The two most important processes in all the textile industries were spinning and weaving, and until the end of the eighteenth century several spinners were needed to supply yarn for one weaver. Women and children were the spinners, and as such it was their employment which was, across the country, the most rapidly growing. There was of course regional specialization in cloth production. The long-established areas included the southwest of England and East Anglia, and the newly growing ones Lancashire and the West Riding of Yorkshire in the first seventy years of the eighteenth century. Yet the continuing search for more spinners meant that women in the more remote areas of the country were likely to find casual work in spinning for the centres of cloth production. The wives and daughters of agricultural labourers, of miners and metalworkers could all be enlisted. Everywhere, in the Pennine dales, in Midland villages and in southern England, as well as in the obvious centres, domestic industry of this kind could be found.

It was the numbers of women and children at home, needing a casual income, which made domestic industry so attractive, and lucrative, to entrepreneurs. Women were the most important part of this rural industrial labour force: they were its cheap labour, for the most part subject to an increasing time discipline in delivery and marketing dates, and to the driving down of piece rates. Spinners were among the lowest paid of workers. It has been argued that in households where men, women and children all worked at the family occupations there was both a greater economic role for women to play, and a fair degree of flexibility in the tasks undertaken by different members of the family. Although weaving was mainly a man's trade, it was not at all unusual for women also to be weavers, either assisting their husbands, or as journeywomen in another's workshop. In the hosiery industry of Leicestershire, for example, families rented knitting frames and all members of the family worked. In a small family the husband might work the frame, the children wind bobbins and the wife seam the stockings; in a larger family the wife or elder son might work a second frame and daughters do the work of seaming. Women were responsible for the training and setting to work of the children: they passed on their own skills, though in an informal and unregulated setting. But we know very little about the internal relationships of such families, or how they were affected by this demand for women's labour.

As the demand for the products of such industry grew, entrepreneurs continued to search for new ways to speed up and cheapen production. The years from 1780 to 1830 were to see major changes both in the mechanization of work and in the ways in which production was organized, though these changes did not necessarily take place simultaneously. The new spinning-jenny, which multiplied the number of spindles which could be used by one spinner, broke through the old productivity bottleneck and was not initially at all incompatible with domestic industry. In Lancashire, at first, women found the early jennies increased efficiency and wages; some writers have called them a 'women's technology', the 'machines of the poor'. But as these jennies grew larger, demonstrating what might be achieved, further new developments in spinning, like Arkwright's water frame (1773), and Samuel Crompton's spinning mule (1779), which worked first by water power and then by steam, took spinning into new and larger factories. Women lost their customary employment. On the whole it was in areas outside the main textile centres that they suffered most; in the remoter areas and in the agricultural south the most important way of earning money for women was being lost. Some older textile areas like the west country could not maintain their impetus against newer competition from northern England, and women there too acutely felt the loss of spinning. A magistrate in Somerset in 1790 was called in to protect the property of two manufacturers 'from the depredations of a lawless banditi of colliers and their wives, for the wives had lost their work to spinning engines' (quoted in Berg, 1985, p. 143).

The loss of spinning, together with the increasing uncertainty

of work on the land, brought grave difficulties to women needing to contribute as before to their family economies. It did not
necessarily mean an immediate end to paid work performed in
the household. Both the availability of cheap labour and the
concerns of philanthropists helped to foster, for instance, the
rapid growth of the straw-plaiting industry from the end of the
eighteenth century in Bedfordshire, Hertfordshire and
Buckinghamshire. There, the assumption that women needed
to contribute to the support of their families was generally
accepted. At Avebury in Wiltshire, when income from spinning
was lost, women first turned to picking stones and road repair-
ing for a parish allowance. An instructress in straw-plaiting was
hired in the following year by the parish officers, and within a
few months nearly a hundred women and children were earning
something from such industries. Other minor regionally based
industries also continued to employ significant numbers of
women and children: glovemaking around Worcester and the
West Midlands, lacemaking in Bedfordshire, Buckinghamshire
and Northamptonshire.

In the major textile areas, women were already weavers in all
branches of textiles. The increase in production brought about
by the new spinning machinery brought a new demand for
weavers. There were, however, some differences in the employment of women and of men. Even before the coming of the
powerloom, newer and larger looms were introduced − the
broad loom, the jacquard loom for silk, and the Dutch engine
loom − and were initially used mainly by men. In Coventry
during the Napoleonic Wars, male weavers went on strike
against a woman working a Dutch loom, but after 1815 women
were more widely employed on this machine, though they still
encountered some opposition. Women weavers were common
in the Yorkshire and west-country woollen trades; and there
they did come to use the more efficient looms.

In the early cotton industry women tended to be employed
as weavers in the less-skilled country branches, still using the
ordinary handloom, while master weavers in the towns used
the Dutch loom in large workshops. But from the 1790s, the
impact of the spinning machinery was such as to create a

massive demand for handloom weavers. There was a huge expansion along the old lines of domestic industry; a new army of outworking weavers, of whom the majority were probably women and children, met this demand. By the 1830s there were estimates of around a quarter of a million cotton weavers in England and Scotland. In some localities we have more detailed figures. In northeast Lancashire, the average household in some of the smaller villages was likely to have two or three looms. All members of the household would have been very actively involved. Again there was a division between town and country: broadly, weaving in the towns was still more likely to be specialized and male dominated, and to maintain restrictions on those entering the trade. In the countryside, plain weaving was more likely to be integrated with other kinds of work. Only by the mid-1820s, with the coming of the power-loom, were handloom weavers seriously threatened in the cotton industry.

In the two branches of the wool industry, domestic industry was much more long-lasting, and factory production and domestic industry continued to coexist for much longer. In the woollen industry (using short-fibred wool) the preparatory processes were mechanized after 1790, but mule-spinning was not extensive until after 1830 and powerloom weaving until after 1850. Again, women became weavers in large numbers from the 1790s, especially on narrow looms, though there were numerous attempts to exclude them or limit their activities. In the worsted industry (using wool with longer fibres) spinning was mechanized from the 1790s, and powerloom weaving was widely introduced from the mid-1830s. In the silk industry, too, women were extensively employed: in the country around Coventry where silk ribbons were produced, there were more women than men employed in the trade. Women had been customarily employed there on single looms in their cottages, and later in workshops in the town — though when the larger looms were introduced even those women who had served apprenticeships were excluded. But after 1815 as more small capitalists entered the industry, looking for cheap labour, women in Coventry too came to work the larger looms. The contrast by the 1820s and 1830s was between women within Coventry who worked, and sometimes owned, their own engine looms, and the countryside, where women worked on the poorly paid single handloom either full-time or casually.

In other industries, too, mechanization brought new divisions of labour in the countryside. In framework knitting in the East Midlands, women had formerly spun the yarn, and men knit the finished stockings on their frames. With the coming of spinning machinery, women came to work on the frames and also became seamers. In Leicestershire and Nottinghamshire villages women worked to seam stockings in their homes, and on the knitting frames at home and in workshops. One witness to the enquiry of the 1840s noted the changes:

As to women, fifty years ago there were very few of them on the frames; but women have been on the increase for a number of years; fifty years ago I knew but one woman in the parish that worked on the frame. (Quoted in Levine, 1977, p. 33)

Yet women in the countryside experienced the impact not only of new technology, but of new ways of organizing production. It is misleading to see new workshops and factories only in the context of the urban world of mid-Victorian England. Such forms had their origins in the cheap labour (as well as the energy sources) of the countryside. There was also the precedent set by the houses of industry established in some parishes to keep the poor occupied. Concentrating workers together in a workshop or factory was a useful strategy for industrialists. So the increasing demand for printed cotton cloths or calicoes led the industrialist Sir Robert Peel to establish long terraces of cottage-like workshops in villages around his mills, where women worked in the delicate and skilled task of calico printing, or handpainting designs. Because this was done by women it was for the most part poorly paid and labour intensive: by setting up such workshops Peel did not have to employ skilled male craftsmen.

In the silk industry the first spinning mill had been set up in

1719, employing some 300 workers, and 'throwing mills', as they were known, spread during the eighteenth century in both towns and countryside, mainly to employ women and children. But by the end of the century industrialists were looking very consciously to the countryside, to avoid having to conform to the regulated wage and piece-rates of the Spitalfields silk-weaving community in London. In particular the availability of the cheap labour of women and girls attracted entrepreneurs to the Essex countryside, which with the decline of the woollen industry and the absence of agricultural employment for women seemed an ideal site for new silk mills. In the late eighteenth century a number of small mills moved out to the Essex villages deliberately to use women's labour. George and Samuel Courtauld set up their first mill in Braintree, using children from the local workhouse as well as women. They followed it with a mill at Bocking, and finally settled in Halstead in 1825. Ten years later they employed nearly 400 employees, three-quarters of whom were women.

Factories then built on existing models, early mills and workshops, using the labour both of women and of men in the most profitable way. There could be differences in organization. Some so-called 'mills' were effectively centralized workshops bringing together all the tasks usually performed in the house-hold. In others, manufacturers employed waged labour to produce cloth, usually with some form of mechanization. In the cotton industry the first small factories were usually small, sometimes bringing together spinning-jennies under a single roof. Only the new Arkwright water frame brought with it the possibility of the greater factories. Small firms coexisted with the giant factories — some multi-storeyed, built for the pur-pose, with clearly structured assembly lines, others collections of small buildings or mere shacks. On the new mule-spinning machines, especially the larger ones, spinning was claimed as a male occupation, fiercely defended. Girls would be employed extensively in these spinning factories as piecers, the assistants to the male workers: they might well be employed as a member of a family, with their father paid the wages for the work of the whole family. Their mothers were more likely to continue in

24

domestic industry; though a minority of women, especially in the years up to 1830, did learn the skills and were quite widely used on the smaller mules. The desirability of this from the employers' point of view was emphasized by their search for what was called a 'self-acting' mule: one which required less skill and strength, and could be run by cheaper women's labour. The most important shift of women into factory production was to develop only from the mid-1820s as the power-loom came to replace the handloom: this is discussed in chapter 3.

The textile industries and associated trades were not the only form of domestic industry in which rural women were engaged. The metal trades of the Black Country were expanding rapidly to meet the demands for exported goods in the eighteenth century. The handmade-nail trade was wholly an outwork industry in this period, with rods of iron handed out to workers who forged and hammered them into nails in their own workshops. By 1830 this particular domestic industry was at its height; from then on it was to decline in the face of urban machine-made competition. But throughout its development women, both married and unmarried, worked alongside men. William Hutton in 1741 reacted strongly to the kind of work that women nailers were doing:

> In some of these shops I observed one, or more females, stript of their upper garment, and not overcharged with their lower, wielding the hammer with all the grace of the sex. The beauties of their face were rather eclipsed by the smut of the anvil ... Struck with the novelty, I enquired, 'whether the ladies of this country shod horses?' but was answered, with a smile, 'they are nailers'. (Quoted in Pinchbeck, 1981, p. 278)

There is evidence of women doing a wide range of such heavy labour in the Black Country metal trades.

Women living in the countryside and in country towns and villages experienced the pressures of significant economic change in this period. Assumptions about women's family roles

25

and about the appropriate division of labour between women and men very much influenced these changes: as we have seen, the massive expansion of production in the eighteenth and early nineteenth centuries arguably owed as much to the use of the cheap labour of women and children as to new technologies. The precise division of labour between men and women in particular industries was still shifting. What was men's work and what was women's work depended on a number of factors: how effectively and cheaply the employment of women and children could replace that of men; how far employers needed certain kinds of skilled artisans, assumed to be men; how strongly male workers defended their own conditions. The boundaries of employment were not only between men and women, of course: there were likely to be very considerable differences, for instance, between the younger urban woman and the married woman living in the country. Nevertheless, before 1830 among women living and working on the land and in industry, the assumption was hardly challenged that women, married and unmarried, young and old, should normally be contributing to the family economy – though many women experienced increasing difficulty in doing so.

## URBAN WOMEN: THE OLD TRADES AND THE NEW INDUSTRIES

In an urban context, given more formal ways of organizing industry, the patterns of male and female work should be seen more clearly, though it is still true that we have little systematic modern research to draw upon for a full picture of such work. The structure of apprenticeship and admission to trades through craft organizations was theoretically controlled by the Statute of Artificers of 1563. London and the older cities, such as Bristol, York, Exeter, Norwich, still inherited the appearance if not the reality of such earlier regulation. From the medieval period, women had been admitted to guilds and were clearly present in the economic life of towns and cities. They worked in a wide range of trades, unconstrained by any fixed ideals of

26

female work. Women were members, for instance, of the London Company of Carmen, working along the docks and warehouses of the Thames, owning their own carts and doing business with them. Apprenticeship records suggest that women were apprenticed to a wide variety of trades, from mantua makers to blacksmiths.

At the same time, their roles were also clearly restricted. Women worked predominantly in occupations connected with textiles, petty retailing and the provision of food and drink. What they did depended partly on their family situation. Married women would most frequently share the labour of their husband's trade or shop; if widowed they were likely to inherit his work and admission to his craft, perhaps then managing a substantial concern or retail business. Women may be found established by this route in a very wide variety of trades: printers, glaziers, plumbers, coal merchants and so on. While married women did sometimes work independently of their husband's occupation, they were very unlikely to have been admitted to any of the crafts of high status. Recent research suggests that while apprenticeship for girls was more common than may have been thought, most such apprenticeships were in female trades, and were unlikely to involve later admission to a guild: Berg writes that 'apprenticeship for girls was about maintenance and general training before marriage, while boys underwent systematic industrial training' (1987, p. 75). The wives of labourers and poorer journeymen, if not employed in their husbands' trades, would still have to contribute to the family income. They might hawk fish or fruit, or porter goods in the market, or sew, clean or take in washing.

Nevertheless in the eighteenth century it remained true that in certain urban trades skilled women workers who had served an apprenticeship were more likely to have their skills recognized, and rewarded by higher wages than might be expected elsewhere. So, in the workrooms of Josiah Wedgwood in London in the 1770s a skilled woman flower painter might expect 3s 6d a day — a high rate for a woman though only two-thirds of the top male rate. For certain tasks in the button-making and toy trades, in painting and decorating in the potteries, in calico printing, such 'female' attributes as delicacy and deftness were looked for. Women silk weavers who had served their apprenticeship and were a part of the urban communities of Spitalfields or Coventry might still earn relatively high wages as journeywomen, or own their own machines.

The older structure of craft organization, however, with admission restricted to those who had served their time, was changing throughout the eighteenth century; and this could affect women in a number of different ways. Guilds of all kinds in corporate towns were losing their control over entry to their crafts from the 1690s to the 1770s. In the early eighteenth century, old established mercers' and drapers' companies in cities such as York and Norwich had fought a losing battle against women setting up as mantua makers, dressmakers and milliners. These changes could make life easier for women as retail traders, especially in areas where they characteristically had a claim – in groceries or the provision trade, for instance.

However, in the major cities the expanding economy required the tradesman or woman to run a substantial business: the need for capital and for a larger workforce must have made the situation more difficult for independent women traders, even in so-called female trades or inherited businesses. Millinery and dressmaking remained mainly women's trades, and smaller shopkeepers at the less formal and capitalized end of the business were frequently women. We have little firm information on the changing situation of women in urban trades by the end of the eighteenth century, though by the 1790s there were several complaints by women writers of the difficulties faced by women in business, given the presence of male competition.

Apprenticeships themselves were becoming shorter, with male apprentices having little prospect of becoming masters themselves. The new relationship was more likely to be that of the master employing a significant number of journeymen and apprentices on a contractual basis rather than on the old basis of an apprentice being taken in and living with the family. By the late eighteenth century the world of the London trades and of many provincial cities was a precarious one, overstocked with trained journeymen. The repeal of the Statute of Artificers in 1814 – against the petitions of masters and journeymen of many trades – reflected rather than created this decline in older urban ways of working.

The response of male journeymen in many trades was to organize to protect their craft against unrestricted entry. Strikes and combinations for wages were increasing in London from the 1760s. Yet there were clear economic advantages for the entrepreneur in taking advantage of an increasingly open market. In particular, in certain trades it could prove advantageous to employ the cheap labour of women and children, in workshops or on a putting-out basis, to substitute for the trained labour of men. The history of the relationship between male and female workers in the old urban centres is that of the collective defence by male workers – sometimes successful, more often not – of their exclusive control of their craft. This might mean direct attempts to exclude women.

The classic instance of this development lies in the tailoring trades. It is possible to see in London even before 1830 how women were entering this business, once a masculine craft, as cheap labour. Such work, conducted in the home or in small workshops, was in future to be labelled 'the sweated trades'. Before the Napoleonic Wars the high level of union organization among tailors had confined women to the female branch of the trades in dressmaking and millinery and a few less reputable workshops. But the huge growth in government contracts for cheap army or navy clothing during the war brought about the development of a new form of putting-out, in which middlemen employed workers, mainly women, to mass-produce garments in their own homes or in workshops. After the war the rising demand for cheaper goods and the obvious availability of women's labour threatened and eventually destroyed male tailors' control. For women the competition for such work meant a constant driving down of rates for the job. Among the needlewomen of London, struggling for survival at the lowest level, it was almost impossible to earn a living wage.

In a different trade, that of printing, the male worker's defence against both the dilution of their skill and mechanization was more successful. The printing trade had been strictly regulated since the sixteenth century, and in London journeymen printers had been able to form a successful union in the 1780s. Historically women had been excluded from the trade except as the wives and daughters of printers. They did, however, have a certain acknowledged role in bookbinding, as the folders and sewers of paper: this was skilled work, earning good money for women, but still did not entitle them to admittance to the union. This meant that they had no means of resisting the dilution of their own trade, as their apprenticeship structure broke down from the 1780s. Even before mechanization, women bookbinders saw the extensive employment of 'learners' and the introduction of piecework into their trade. And in the future the advantages were all to lie with the male printers' union.

The picture was of course a rather different one in towns which were new and rapidly responding to economic developments. In urban areas which did not enjoy corporate status, where city governments and guilds had never taken root, like Birmingham and the towns and villages of the West Midlands, women were actively involved in the hardware and metal trades. These trades were organized partly in large workshops but also in small household workshops. There was a considerable demand for the products of these trades, which included small metal goods of all kinds, from the expanding nailmaking business to luxury goods like clocks, bronze ornamental work, buttons, lamps, candlesticks, buckles. In the workshops producing such goods there were constantly changing divisions of labour, and adaptation to new methods. In the first half of the nineteenth century the labour of women and children was increasingly being substituted for men: this was a part of the continuing growth of an already dynamic industry. In some of the button factories of Birmingham in the late eighteenth century women already were in the majority and apprenticeship customs were largely ignored. An advertisement for a button burnisher in 1788 called for:

a woman that has been used to looking over and carding plain, plated and gilted buttons, also a few women that have been used to grind steels, either at foot lathes or mill. (Quoted in Berg, 1985, p. 311)

Women were actively sought for the japanning or lacquering trade, where the delicate work was seen as their particular province. New machinery in the late eighteenth century for stamping and piercing metal seemed to extend the tasks for which women were required. By the early nineteenth century, women were still employed in a wide range of processes, but increasingly in the less skilled and newer branches.

For girls and young women, especially those coming to the city for the first time, one likely occupation in the early nineteenth century was to be in a form of domestic service. At the lowest level the girl from the workhouse might be bound to be the domestic drudge of a poor family. Clearly many such servants in the small households of shopkeepers and tradesmen were likely to turn their hands to whatever work was required of them, not limiting themselves to cooking, cleaning and washing, but perhaps also serving in the shop or assisting at the workbench. Apprenticeship under such circumstances meant little. Nevertheless the domestic and female nature of such service was receiving more attention. The country girl seeking employment as a servant in London was known to be vulnerable to seduction and prostitution: but the huge growth of London in the eighteenth and early nineteenth centuries, and its attractions for the wealthy as the greatest commercial and social centre in Europe, meant a continuing demand for the domestic labour of women, both as living-in servants and as casual workers. The nature of their work is discussed in chapter 4.

This was, however, much less the case in other urban areas where female migration was also extensive: those which were growing rapidly on the basis of the new textile industries, in Lancashire and Yorkshire. The population of Manchester and Salford had grown from around 30,000 in 1775 to 84,000 in 1801, and in areas such as the Black Country, southeastern

Lancashire, the West Riding of Yorkshire and the East Midlands, urban expansion continued. But by 1801 outside London there were still only five cities in England and Wales with populations over 50,000: Birmingham, Manchester, Leeds, Liverpool and Bristol. Though one-third of the population in this period lived in an 'urban' environment (measured according to those living in communities of over 10,000) the early industrial towns were still mainly small communities with close links to their rural industrial surroundings.

Women migrants came mainly from that surrounding countryside; there was also substantial Irish immigration into Lancashire. In families which came to the spinning factories for work, a father might work as a mule-spinner, the children acting as piecers to him or others. The wife and mother might remain in domestic industry, or be involved in the factory, in the preparatory processes or as spinners on the smaller mules. The expansion and mechanization of the lacemaking industry at Nottingham attracted women and men both into the factories and to the finishing that could be done as outwork. Women came to find work in Leeds as the expansion of the worsted trades brought a new level of demand for domestic weavers. These new areas of urban growth, built largely upon the textile industries, utilized cheap labour, new technology and new methods of production. Domestic industry and the new factories coexisted, feeding each other. Only from the mid-1820s, as weaving itself was mechanized, was there a substantial and growing demand for adult women workers in factory production; this is discussed below in chapter 3.

What has been emphasized in this survey of the changing patterns of women's paid work in the period from 1750 to 1830 has been the part which women's cheap labour, used in diverse ways, played in the process of industrialization. Such labour was as attractive and as essential in this process as new technology. To understand why women's labour had such distinctive characteristics, we should turn to look not only at women's paid work, but at the division of labour between women and men within the family.

# 2

## Women, the Family and Economic Change 1750–1830

The period from 1750 to 1880 saw significant, if gradual, changes in the history of the family, both working-class and middle-class. This does not mean simply the appearance of the 'Victorian family'. These changes began far earlier, and should be seen in relation to the growth of wealth and population which developed throughout the eighteenth century.

Source materials for the study of the family are diverse. Legal records of church and criminal courts may tell us about the distribution of property within families, and about separation, divorce and conflict; containing much vital material, they are as yet under-used by historians of this period. Most progress has been made in the field of demography, where economic historians have been able to use quantitative methods to reconstruct both the family history of individual parishes and the likely patterns of birth, marriage and death in the population as a whole. Quantitative methods have proved important too in analyses of census material after 1851, from which more detailed reconstruction of family histories has proved possible. Yet perhaps the majority of writers have tended to rely on qualitative evidence: diaries, autobiographies, correspondence, prescriptive writings. There can be dangers here: to generalize about relationships between husbands and wives, mothers and children, from a scattered range of material, to prove a particular thesis, invites criticism. Professor Lawrence Stone's work *The Family, Sex and Marriage in England 1500–1800* (1977) provoked much hostility for that very reason. But when qualitative material is clearly anchored in its context, whether that of a particular family history, or of a group clearly situated in class, locality or religion, it is likely to prove the most illuminating source of all. Such qualitative material is of course extremely difficult to find except among the literate and comfortably off. A recent study of working-class autobiographies covering the period between 1790 and 1850, David Vincent's *Bread, Knowledge and Freedom* (1981), found only six autobiographies by women, out of a total of 142.

Formally, for all classes and conditions of women and men, family relationships were ultimately determined by the law; and family law in mid-eighteenth-century England was a very complex business. It was regulated by three different kinds of law. The common law, inherited from the medieval period, depended on custom, precedent and past practice. It was amended from time to time by new statute law or new legislation affecting the family, such as Lord Hardwicke's Act of 1754, intended to ensure a more formal structure of marriage. This prescribed that all marriages had to take place in church, with the banns called, and eliminated the possibility of clandestine marriage. The law of equity, a relatively new development, was practised in the Court of Chancery, which dealt mainly with contractual and financial matters. Ecclesiastical law, practised in the church courts, governed the annulment of marriages, the separation of husbands and wives, and also disputed wills.

The structures of authority within the family were governed by common law, which could be seen as a truly patriarchal instrument. The leading eighteenth-century legal commentator, Sir William Blackstone, wrote of the relations between husband and wife:

By marriage the husband and wife are one person in law; that is, the very being or legal existence of the woman is suspended during the marriage, or at least is incorporated and consolidated into that of the husband. (1771, vol. 1, p. 442)

A wife's property passed into the hands of her husband on marriage: he became the absolute owner of all her personal property, and guardian of any landed property she possessed. A wife could not sue or be sued and had no civil legal personality in her own right. The law regarded a husband as his wife's guardian, and he had the right to control her actions and even chastise her 'with a stick no thicker than his thumb'. A husband had the absolute right to custody of the children, and the wife no rights at all over them.

The harshness of the common law was to some extent mediated by other forms of law. For well-to-do families — for whom a husband's right to property might mean a daughter would lose any gifts given to her on marriage — it was possible to use the law of equity to protect a wife's money in complex and unbreakable financial trusts. By the late eighteenth century women of the landed and wealthy classes normally enjoyed this kind of protection of their property. An appeal to ecclesiastical law through the church courts was the only formal legal means by which a woman separated from or deserted by her husband might claim some form of maintenance from him. The only possibility of a divorce in this period, before the Divorce Act of 1857, was to introduce a Private Bill into the House of Lords: only four women ever achieved that. Alternatively a poor woman could appeal only to the Poor Law authorities for relief.

These structures were complicated and chaotic. They rested on the survival of the pre-Reformation ecclesiastical law and on a common law which was itself disordered and generally recognized in this context as outdated. Just as the wealthier classes used the law of equity to circumvent the harshness of the common law, so different classes and conditions of women and men inherited and adapted their own conventions of family life. These informal conventions were likely to shape women's experience more closely than any distant authority. Nevertheless the oppressive character of the common law continued to bear harshly on women who were poor, who were unprotected by family or community or who dared to break with local or family custom.

The familiar picture of the pattern of marriage in early modern
England among the working population is one of marriage at a
fairly late age, perhaps at twenty-five to twenty-seven. While
working men and women were relatively free to choose their
own partners, likely to be from those in a similar walk of life,
they would need to prepare their route to marriage: this might
mean serving out one's time as an apprentice, or saving money
as a farm or domestic servant, or as a journeyman or woman.
Women and men were not only marrying but also establishing
a family economy: they had to look to their own future and to
that of their children, in trade, shop or cottage. It was a world
in which attraction between women and men had to be bal-
anced – though not eliminated – by sensible judgements
about the future.

Quantitative historians have recently looked closely at the
outlines of family history, and indirectly therefore at the lives of
women in the family. While the broad outline of this pattern of
late marriage continued, there were some significant variations
within it. Population historians noted that these years were
those of massive population growth: the best estimates are that
the population of England rose from 5,772,000 in 1751 to
13,284,000 in 1831. This increase in population arose more
from a significant increase in fertility rates than from any
startling fall in mortality. From a detailed study of twelve
English parishes, the demographers E. T. Wrigley and R. S.
Schofield suggested that there was little sign of any overall
increase in fertility in marriage: that is, there was no indication
that women were having children more frequently once married.
The increase in fertility was to be explained in two other ways:
more women and men were marrying, at an earlier age, and –
of lesser importance – the number of children born outside
marriage was increasing.

The most important change was that more women and men
were marrying and they were marrying at a younger age. From
the twelve parishes studied we can see that the average age at

marriage for women in 1700—24 was 26.9; for the quarter century 1800—24 it was 23.7. There had been a steady fall in the age at which marriage took place for both women and men, though it was slightly more marked for women. Again according to the same evidence, in 1700 approximately 15 per cent of women and men never married. By 1771 that figure had fallen to just over 5 per cent and remained at under 10 per cent for this period. At the same time, the number of children born outside wedlock and the number of prenuptial pregnancies were also rising. It seems that women were not only marrying earlier, but also starting their childbearing years at an earlier date: for many rural communities at this period having an illegitimate child did not exclude a future marriage, and a pregnancy might well mean community pressure on a couple to get married.

From this evidence, it would seem that marriage had never been so popular. We need to build upon these rather bare indications of change to understand the kind of balance that could exist by the end of our period between the family as a place of emotional fulfilment and as an economic unit. We can look at the interaction between family lives and economic shifts and at the place of marriage within different communities — and finally we should consider what one historian has termed the 'romantic revolution' of this period.

The changing patterns of women's and men's work may have significantly affected decisions about when to get married or set up a household. Much of the work now being done on the correlation between economic and demographic patterns is speculative, but suggestive. The older system of marriage in the late twenties for women and men had conformed to a world in which living in service was a normal part of rural life. The change to employing male labourers could bring everyone much greater freedom to court and marry at an earlier age. But the decision to marry would also be influenced by the likely cost of establishing a home and bringing up a family. In the southern and eastern parts of the country those costs might seem a deterrent, given the high price of bread in relation to wages by the end of the eighteenth century; but employers

37

were coming to prefer married labourers, tied to a low-paid job, providing also the casual work of wife and children when required. As regular work for single women labourers declined, women were more likely to gain casual work on the land once married. The system of poor relief prevailing until 1834 offered outdoor relief, but discriminated for all the above reasons in favour of the married. There seem to have been real economic incentives towards marrying younger in these arable regions.

In areas where agricultural work was combined with a growing domestic industry, patterns were also changing but for different reasons. There the family remained an important unit of production, with probably the whole family or at least some of it working for piece rates as producers, in weaving, framework knitting, mining. The labour and earnings of all members of a family including wife and children was important – and it has been argued that this also encouraged early marriage and childbearing, though the argument remains a controversial one. For some historians it implies too conscious or calculating a mentality on the part of weaving or knitting families: earlier marriage can be explained rather by an increasing general level of material prosperity. A similar freedom to marry early would be enjoyed by the workers in the early cotton mills, enjoying the benefits of wages high by contemporary standards.

Yet there is considerable evidence overall of the relationship between occupation and family formation. In urban communities in the mid-eighteenth century, it still remained true that a lengthy apprenticeship or period of domestic service would be necessary before a prudent and sensible couple might enter into their own trade or shop. Those living within the city, both native and immigrant, still tended to marry later. For the modestly prosperous shopkeeping and trading class, this remained true throughout this period, though delay in marriage was also reinforced by ideas about what was respectable. But elsewhere the undermining of older craft controls – notably in London – brought a family economy dependent on a combination of wages and putting-out systems. So combining the efforts of husband and wife, struggling to survive together in a hostile city, with or without a formal marriage, could seem the best way forward.

We tend to think of the decision as to whether or not to marry as a private decision, relevant only to the two people concerned and their families. In the eighteenth and early nineteenth centuries that decision was not necessarily such a private one. Courtship, marriage or common-law union and the later relationship between husband and wife were all matters on which the broader community in which women and men lived might have its own conventions, perhaps very different from formal legal structures. Much depended on how close-knit and independent of authority such communities were. In early modern England, where young men and women lived and worked relatively independently but with their own sex for a considerable period before marriage, courtship might be conducted publicly, and betrothal, the agreement to marry, would be undertaken normally in the presence of friends. If betrothal was followed by making love, that could be understood as committing the couple to marriage. And marriage had its own important rites, initiating the new household. The church service could be less important than the wedding party, the toasting, feasting and distribution of favours. In Yorkshire there was a traditional and lively race from the church to the bride's house with the winner gaining the prize of the bride's garter. Sometimes the church door would be barred, with the couple paying a penalty to come out. Villages, and urban crafts, had their own ways of initiating members to married life.

These ways of getting married were becoming much less common by the early nineteenth century; and the reasons tell us something about the balance between family, community and authority, which had its own consequences for women. For the middle and upper classes, these were years in which family ideals and the concept of an ordered society were being reshaped. Local custom especially when at odds with the church, which might hold different views of marriage, had to be controlled and restrained – ultimately, it was to give way to a national pattern. In the rural south and east, both the older patterns of courtship and the big public wedding were eroded more rapidly. For those dependent on wage labour, with no property or trade skills, the festivities associated with the big wedding, initiating the new household, were luxuries that could not be afforded. The couple and friends were more likely to walk to the church on their wedding morning and return to work again.

Elsewhere, where domestic industry and smallholding survived longer, the big wedding might be a focus for conflict. In the Yorkshire Dales, for instance, there were continuous conflicts between the clergy and gentry on the one hand, and communities on the other, over the race for the bride's garter. It was actively defended both by Yorkshire women and by the craftsmen and smallholders of local villages: as one woman defended it to the local parson's wife in Bedale in 1812:

> Ah allus kept mahsel respectable, an mah mother war reckoned to yan o't maist respectablest women 'at anybody ivver clapped 'e's on an' er garter was raced for.
> (Quoted in Gillis, 1985, p. 147)

The strong local community might, however, defend not only such customs but also distinctive structures of sexual relationships. In communities dependent on the textile industry or other forms of family industry, women's earning power was likely to be sought after early. There was much intermarriage in weaving, mining and smithing communities. Courtship retained its importance, and the practice of night visiting or 'bundling' (when couples courted by spending the night together, though not necessarily having intercourse) was still fairly common. And there was nothing at all unusual in a majority of rural communities about sex before marriage or premarital pregnancy. In one area of Dorset, the Isle of Portland, men and women did not marry until the woman became pregnant:

> The mode of courtship here, is that a young woman never admits of the serious addresses of a young man but on the

supposition of a thorough probation. When she becomes with child, she tells her mother; the mother tells her father; her father tells his father, and he tells his son, that it is then proper time to be married ... If the woman does not prove with child, after a competent time of courtship, they conclude they are not destined by Providence for each other; they therefore separate ... (Quoted in Gillis, 1985, p. 126)

The pressure of families, peer groups and communities to marry in such a situation could be reinforced by Poor Law authorities' readiness to charge the father of illegitimate children maintenance for them.

In some communities cohabitation was common and accepted. In some areas of Wales the 'besom wedding' — where a couple jumped over a broom at the threshold of their house, in the sight of witnesses — was still acknowledged in the late eighteenth century, perhaps later. Among London shoemakers and costermongers, couples 'married' by exchanging handkerchiefs or other tokens. Those who lived outside marriage were by no means simply the poor or vagrant. In Culcheth, a South Lancashire cotton handloom-weaving village, the growth both of cohabitation and illegitimacy coincided precisely with the growth of the new domestic industry, and no stigma was attached to either. In communities, sometimes remote ones, where there were common economic roots and a habit of dissent, not marrying was a challenge to authority which did not bring with it local condemnation of any irregularity. The same assumptions could govern the behaviour of immigrants to London: the records of the London Foundling Hospital suggest that sexual intimacy was normal once marriage had been promised, and that a date for marriage would be set though circumstances see it pass without a ceremony. Domestic servants would try to conceal their pregnancies; women working in trades would simply cohabit. All this was consistent with the older practice of betrothal: intercourse implied commitment to marriage. And women in this position might be seen as keeping a greater freedom practically and legally: they might require maintenance of their children if marriage were to fall through, and they did still retain control over their property.

The community was interested not only in the way households were set up but also in how they were maintained, or in the last resort broken up. There were, and had been for centuries, ways in which disapproval of notorious behaviour could be made clear. Local crowds might demonstrate by 'rough music', shouting, beating on pans, blowing on horns and whatever else came to hand, outside the offender's house. In early modern England such demonstrations could be directed against the woman who was a scold or who henpecked her husband or was unfaithful. The husband should be seen to rule in his household, though he too had to observe certain standards. But in the course of the eighteenth century the targets changed: such local demonstrations were as often directed against husbands who beat their wives unreasonably or were notorious adulterers. As far as is known such 'rough music' was made mainly in rural districts: it was clearly declining by the mid-nineteenth century, though isolated examples are still cited by historians.

Another informal convention was that used by those who were married, separated and wanted to marry again. The new regulation of marriage since 1753 prevented any further church ceremony, and no divorce was yet possible. In the eighteenth and nineteenth centuries recourse was made to a distinctive set of conventions by which couples might divorce themselves, the release from their former partner enabling them to marry again. The process could be begun by man or woman, but both had to agree to the ending of all marital obligations, of maintenance by the man and earnings and obedience from the woman. The rite was mutually agreed − and not what it appeared. So George Hitchinson of Burntwood in Staffordshire brought his wife to Walsall Market in 1837:

They came into the market between ten and eleven o'clock in the morning, the woman being led by a halter, which was fastened round her neck and the middle of her body. In a few minutes after their arival she was sold to a man of the name of Thomas Snape, a nailer, also of Burntwood. There were not many people in the market at the time. The purchase money was 2s 6d and all the parties seemed satisfied with the bargain. The husband was glad to get rid of his frail rib, who it seems had been living with Snape three years ... (Quoted in Gillis, 1985, p. 213)

Wife-sale meant the public acknowledgement of this form of divorce, a just and legal ending of mutual obligations. It is difficult to know how widespread it was: one historian has located 294 instances between 1780 and 1880 (Menefee, 1981).

In any discussion of the relationship between economic change and family lives, it is important to avoid simple correlations. This was a world in which infant mortality rates were high, and where marriages were intensely vulnerable to death and to separation. Economic considerations did shape the choice of partner, the time of marriage, and perhaps influenced childbearing too. But we should not assume that such considerations eliminated sexual attraction and the desire for affection and companionship between women and men; nor did an awareness of the dangers facing small infants prevent mothers caring for their children and grieving deeply at their loss. Evidence of the feelings of working-class women, their balance of expectations, is scanty. The ceremony of marriage should not be seen as the culmination of romantic expectations in the twentieth-century sense; but continuing shared hopes for a joint and loving future could and did exist, if not undermined and eroded by the harshest of circumstances.

The above should suggest that in a variety of ways marriage and family relations among the working classes did not by 1830 conform to any image of the private and domesticated family of which Queen Victoria was herself to be the symbol. Sexual relations outside marriage were common; marriage itself was undertaken for material as well as emotional reasons; the formation of a household was a public as well as a private affair. Economic changes – especially the coming of domestic industry – might encourage early marriage, but they had not yet undermined the assumptions of the family economy. Within the wealthier classes, however, a new image and a new practice of family relations was being shaped.


## MIDDLE-CLASS WOMEN AND THE SHAPING OF THE PRE-VICTORIAN FAMILY: DOMESTIC IDEOLOGY

The middle classes were growing both in numbers and influence during this period. They developed and looked to new forms of commercial, industrial and professional wealth and income. Though the aristocracy and gentry too were extensively involved in such new forms, those in the middle ranks were to depend most heavily upon, and to be identified with, these new sources of wealth. It is extremely difficult and controversial to define the membership of the middle classes in this period: probably an income of £200 to £300 would earn a place within the lower ranks of this group. This could include families drawing their income from professional and mercantile activities, manufacturing families in the north and Midlands, tradesmen, farmers and solicitors in country market towns. It is important to remember that within the middle classes would be many whose lifestyles were modest and frugal. Divisions would include that between the Anglican and the nonconformist (Methodist, Baptist, Independent, Quaker). Some sections of the middle class took a stance in opposition to establishment and government, other would clearly identify with loyalty to Church and King.

For important sections within these middle ranks, it was important to establish a clear and separate identity, an ordered way of life distinct on the one hand from the luxury of the landed classes, and on the other from the disorderly life of the working population. Central to this was a clear concept of the desirability of the private and domesticated family world, apart from the public world of the economic and political marketplace, inspired by moral and religious principles. Of course the development of such a concept was not a straightforward or simple matter: there were many differences of economic interest and many lines of political division. Yet from diverse viewpoints members of the provincial middle classes continued to discuss the proper and separate roles of women and men in a changing social order. Evangelical writing, from different denominations, was particularly powerful in shaping these ideas. Such discussion was accompanied by changes in practice, including the withdrawal of women of the middle classes from many of the productive tasks they might previously have performed.

This new view of the family had a number of different elements within it. First, it was built on the gradual construction of the different spheres occupied by women and by men: indeed it redefined the very meaning of masculinity and femininity. The middle-class man no longer lived by the aristocratic or gentry codes, directed by honour: he needed to justify a new involvement in trade and commerce by his seriousness, uprightness and respectability. Women, however, were no longer to be involved in such activities but were to confine themselves to the private life of home and children: their sphere was dependent and subordinate, though women had some power within their own sphere of the household. Such a viewpoint had of course been expressed before in a variety of contexts. Yet by the late eighteenth and early nineteenth century it had more powerful and dynamic exponents than ever before in England.

The conservative and Anglican evangelical Hannah More has been quoted above. Her novel *Coelebs in search of a wife* (1809) describes a bachelor's search for his ideal woman, found eventually living in her rural retreat, committed to religious and philanthropic works. Later writers echoed that message. One of the most popular Biblical texts quoted by evangelical writers was Ephesians 5:22:

Wives, submit yourselves unto your own husbands, as unto the Lord. For the husband is the head of the wife, even as Christ is the head of the Church: and he is the saviour of the body. Therefore as the church is subject unto Christ, so let the wives be to their own husbands in everything.

One prolific writer and preacher, the Independent clergyman John Angell James, expounded this text: for him the wife and mother 'must be a *keeper at home* to fulfil her duties' (quoted in Rendall, 1985, p. 76). The messages came not only from the clergy. A popular writer of simple poetry, Ann Taylor Gilbert, whose best-known poem was 'Twinkle Twinkle Little Star', also published in 1812 her 'Remonstrance':

> *His* soul is thoughtful and profound;
> *Hers*, brilliant and acute; —
> Plants cultured, each, in different ground
> And bearing different fruit.
>
> Among the social duties led,
> Where each excels in part,
> Man's proudest glory is his head,
> A Woman's, is her heart.
>
> Unwearied in the toilsome course,
> *He* climbs the hill of fame;
> Takes immortality by force,
> And wins a mighty name.
>
> Along a cool sequestered way,
> *Her* quiet walk she winds;
> Sheds milder sunshine on his day,
> His brow with flowers binds.
>
> Of art intuitive possest,
> Her infant train she rears;
> To virtue by her smiles carest,
> Or chastened by her tears... (Quoted in
> Davidoff and Hall, 1987, pp. 455–8)

Here the clear separation of the future paths of men and women is accompanied by the very different qualities associated with masculinity and femininity.

With this separation of worlds came an idealization, even a redefinition, of motherhood, seen in the last verse of this poem. Educational writers from the late eighteenth century – Hannah More, the novelist Maria Edgeworth, the Scottish writer Elizabeth Hamilton – had all emphasized the importance of a mother's role in shaping the world of the infant and small child: with the mother lay the responsibility for the first early direction of moral and religious character. Edgeworth in particular, in *Practical Education* (1798), offered a child-centred ideal of education, aiming to draw out the child's natural curiosity and abilities. Even the feminist Mary Wollstonecraft, though disagreeing with these writers on many points, also laid strong emphasis on the importance of motherhood, as the 'peculiar destination' of women offering a 'dignified domestic happiness'. Others, like Ann Taylor Gilbert, popularized these ideas in the first decades of the nineteenth century in both poetry and prose.

A further assumption in Ann Taylor Gilbert's poem was the association between women and 'virtue'. The literature of the period emphasizes women's potential for moral superiority. Women were identified more with the heart than with the head, again as suggested in the poem, with feeling rather than with reason, as more likely to be sustained by faith and belief and as closer to God. For one leading figure of the Anglican evangelical movement, William Wilberforce, women were: 'the medium of our intercourse with the heavenly world, the faithful repositories of the religious principle for the benefit of the present and of the rising generation' (1797, p. 435). They had a 'more favourable disposition to religion'. This theme is a recurring one, shared by all denominations alike. The evangelical message was a dynamic one, which called for the converted to battle against sin in all its forms. Women might therefore be seen to have a particular mission in this battle. The first battleground was clearly the home. But beyond that women might take their moral strength and their religious mission to a wider world, in educating, visiting and reforming the poor and unfortunate. Philanthropy could be seen as an extension of the domestic world and therefore an activity permitted to women.

Finally, along with this potential for moral superiority went the cultivation of gentility, delicacy and refinement, and a denial of all that went counter to a growing emphasis on refined behaviour. Most notable, and notorious as 'Victorian', was the denial by and to women of any awareness of sexual passion. Changing standards of propriety in public life were already apparent some years before the accession of Queen Victoria. From the 1790s onwards evangelicals campaigned for a reform of manners and morals, partly through such societies as the Society for the Suppression of Vice. They directed their fire against the bawdiness associated with the world of the Regency and the sexual licence of some sections of the aristocracy. A new literature, directed at the middle-class family, controlling and limiting awareness of sexuality, was growing. Thomas Bowdler's *Family Shakespeare*, a purified version which took out all sexual and bawdy references, first appeared in 1818, giving the verb 'to bowdlerize' to the language. Evangelical campaigners expected similar standards of morality and behaviour from men and women; but particular emphasis was laid on the innocence and purity of mind expected of young girls and women, to be preserved only through safeguarding them from any knowledge of sexuality.

In the trial of Queen Caroline in 1820 the clash of moralities was made public. On his accession, the new King George, formerly the Prince Regent, had declared his intention to divorce his Queen from whom he had long been separated, and accused her of adultery in spite of his own numerous and flagrant infidelities. The public saw Queen Caroline as a wronged woman, a virtuous heroine, a victim of her licentious husband. This was in fact all very unconvincing, since she too had led a relaxed and often indiscreet life abroad; nevertheless even Caroline did briefly become a symbol for those defending domestic values and sexual morality. After 1830, similarly, King William and Queen Adelaide were celebrated for the quiet domesticity of their Court. Queen Victoria was to meet an already existing demand for such a symbol.

One consequence of this new morality may have been that it was easier for friendship and love to be expressed between women, if women were seen as lacking in, or without awareness

of, any sexual feeling. Certainly we know that romantic friend-
ships between women of the upper and middle classes could
provide them with emotional support and intimacy. For a few,
like Lady Eleanor Butler and Sarah Ponsonby, the 'Ladies of
Llangollen', who lived together for many years, such friendship
meant the possibility of a different way of life. On the other
hand, a diary kept by Anne Lister of Halifax in the 1830s,
much of it written in code and only recently deciphered, offers
a portrait of a young woman from the gentry class who was
clearly sexually attracted to women: but her lesbianism was
recognized, and aroused hostility in her own community. We
still know very little about the relationship between the apparently rigid codes of 'Victorian' behaviour and the sexual
lives of women and men.

### DOMESTIC PRACTICE IN THE MIDDLE-CLASS FAMILY

Prescriptive ideology does not necessarily tell us very much
about what was going on in the middle-class family in these
years of social and economic change. To understand that, we
have to look more carefully at what evidence is available. It
would seem that the economic changes indicated in chapter 1
did have important consequences for middle-class women, in
that they were in 1830 less likely than in 1750 to take an active
part in the family enterprise; this remained, however, a tran-
sitional period in which regional differences are still important,
and our sources limited. This did not mean, however, that the
ties of family did not have important economic functions; these
have been recently analysed by Leonore Davidoff and Catherine
Hall.

Davidoff and Hall have illustrated the changing relationship
of middle-class women to the family business by looking at two
generations of the Cadbury family. In 1796 Richard Cadbury,
with a drapery business in the centre of Birmingham, married
his wife Elizabeth; they lived over the shop. For the next
fourteen years Elizabeth not only bore ten children and ran a
household but played an important role in the background of
the business: she had always to be ready to serve in the shop,

supervise the apprentices and oversee all in her husband's absence. Her sons and daughters as they grew up were also expected to play their parts. From 1812 onwards they rented a second house in the pleasant suburb of Edgbaston and there they retired in 1829. Their sons, marrying in 1829 and 1832, spent a few years living over the shop but rapidly moved their families out to Edgbaston. The daughters-in-law of Elizabeth Cadbury were to be preoccupied with domestic affairs, with no active overseeing of the business. Yet the enterprise was still a family affair in the sense that it supported a large family and was managed, and owned, only by family members.

Another example of such a progression might be the female members of the Courtauld family. When Samuel Courtauld first set up his Essex silk-weaving mills in Bocking in 1817 and Halstead in 1825, his sisters acted as overseers of the women weavers – though by the mid-1820s there was already much discussion of the suitability of this work, and after a few years they ceased to play any part in the mill. For the wives and daughters of most manufacturers after 1830 there would be little to do. There were of course always exceptions to this, like the remarkable Lady Charlotte Bertie, who, marrying the iron-master John Guest of Merthyr Tydfil in 1833, took an active interest in the business for twenty years and on his death took over its running.

These changes in the lives of different generations of women are of course related to the difficulties faced by women in urban trades and on the land, noted in chapter 1. Within the families of small tradesmen and of shopkeepers, women may well have continued to assist in the work of an enterprise as before; yet where success brought expansion and financial rewards, they were more likely to retreat into the purely do-mestic household. The industries of the Cadburies, Courtaulds and Guests are of course success stories; we have less in-formation on those who continued in a modest way of life, in the lower middle classes as before. The typing of some tasks as male, others as female, could mean that women were less likely to assist their husbands or succeed them in the kind of work they may have done in the eighteenth century: in farming, for instance, or the building trades. A small family business might be manageable, but the controlling of a labour force and dealing with financial institutions would conflict with expectations of female behaviour. The growth of more formal barriers to the professions meant too that a woman was unlikely to be able to continue to assist or take over a husband's business as doctor or dentist. The expectations developing in the course of the first half of the nineteenth century were that women would be actively involved in economic affairs only out of necessity, if they had neither an income nor husband or father for support.

Nevertheless the reality was not always so clear: there remained ways in which, unobtrusively and acceptably, women might make their contributions. Not only wives but daughters, sisters, mothers and others might put capital directly into a business. So George Courtauld borrowed lump sums from a sister and female friend in the early days in Essex, and used his bride's marriage portion to support them both; later the same bride, now the mother of Samuel Courtauld, assisted her son financially. Some women went on keeping the books and maintaining the correspondence. Above all, they brought up the next generation in the awareness of the importance of the family enterprise, maintained the links of friendship and kinship which might provide goodwill, and perhaps looked too for marriage partners for sons and daughters who would further family interests. Some wives might still make some independent contribution, earning small sums through such activities as dressmaking, teaching, writing. There were less common possibilities. John Constable's sister Ann bred dogs. Others might act as agents for goods and services, make jam or sell engravings.

For single women, the difficulties of surviving independently while not breaching convention were considerable. In the sample of Birmingham and Essex censuses studied by Davidoff and Hall, which allow knowledge only of the occupations of widows and spinsters, the largest group of those recorded in active occupations were professionals – mainly teachers. Teaching remained the first recourse for women forced to support themselves. It could be seen too as a proper extension of a familial and maternal role. The prominence of the governess in early Victorian literature reflected the reality of this as the only option for so many single or widowed women, from the best-known, Mary Wollstonecraft and the Brontës, to many unknown women. There were different possibilities. To become a governess might be socially acceptable, but would be poorly paid and lack status in another's household. Some women were enterprising: Sarah Bache in Birmingham, using her Unitarian connections, established from nothing a small but successful school, with over sixty pupils. Single women might find in running such a school a possible way in which women might live acceptably together, as did Miss Wood and Miss Pirie of Edinburgh, before the mother of one of their pupils spread the rumour that their relationship was 'unnatural' (Faderman, 1981, pp. 147–53). Women often tended to run small day-schools rather than boarding establishments, using other female family labour, especially sisters. On the fringes of the middle classes, some schoolmistresses taught for the new elementary schools founded by the National or British and Foreign Societies: these too were poorly paid.

Other occupations might include running an inn, public house or lodging house. These were important occupations for widows, though growing social disapproval of public drinking places could face such women with problems. The coming of the railways ended the transport connections of such inns, but the provision of food and lodging remained an important resource for lower-middle-class women. So too, as suggested above, did small-scale trading, especially what were thought of as female trades – dressmaking, millinery and food retailing.

Although the growing scale of business enterprises and the ideology of separate spheres could confine the activities of married middle-class women to domesticity, it should be remembered that business still remained very much a family affair. First, before the coming of limited liability, enterprises were personal ones. The entrepreneur with wife, children, servants and employees performed all tasks, took all risks and would be liable for all debts: if the business was to expand, he took a partner, who would be similarly responsible. There was no structure of shareholding until after the Limited Liability Acts of 1856/7, which limited the personal responsibilities of

shareholders. The future of the entrepreneur and of his wif
and children was entirely dependent on the enterprise: there
was as yet no financial separation between home and workplace. In the fiction of the period, the young woman whose
family was ruined by unlucky speculation was a stock figure: in
reality women with few other means of earning a living were
intensely vulnerable to the shifts in trade and the market.

The personal nature of business was set within an environment of kinship, friendship and community. This might be
religious — the strength of Quaker and Unitarian networks was
well known — or simply personal. Friends and kin offered
important resources for advancing business activities through
their connections and interests. The most important of opportunities offered came through marriage. Young women and
men were likely to have a choice of marriage partner but within
a carefully controlled network: a religious community or group
of like-minded families. And the possibility of a partnership or
of tying together two businesses or bringing new expertise into
a family might well be important considerations for both man
and woman. Davidoff and Hall cite among many other instances
that of Samuel Kenrick, taken by his uncle Archibald into the
buckle business when his own sons were too young to help. In
1811 Samuel was offered a choice between becoming a salaried
clerk or a partner. He opted for a partnership and cemented
the relatonship by marrying his cousin, Marianne, who was, of
course, also his senior partner's daughter (Davidoff and Hall,
1987, p. 219).

Women's marriages, while reflecting a choice of partner,
were normally made within particular occupational groups or
communities, and could reflect family aspirations for business
or professional status. Yet it could also be possible within this
framework for young women to make their choice and to take
some initiative in expressing their feelings. In their diaries and
correspondence, young women might express their affections
and expectations for the future: as Eliza Florance wrote to her
future husband, the Rev W. J. Fox, in 1819:

It seems a long time since I heard from, and I cannot tell

how long since I saw you, but while I am stationary here, I cannot imagine how you felt, whose mind is continually drawn to other scenes of activity and usefulness, of gaiety and pleasure. But such, of course, it must ever be with men. Affection and love with them can only be an amusement, a recreation from the business of life; with woman 'tis her life, her breath, her daily food, looking forward, as I have for so many years, to one distinct object ... (Fox, 1869, p. 220)

The first phase of economic change brought for middle-class women the gradual appearance of a new kind of division between the public and private worlds, between home and work. For most married women, economic expansion and success in the family enterprise brought the expectation of, and often aspirations towards, domesticity. For the widowed and single, the picture is far less clear, but a narrowing of occupational possibilities was to be combined with an increased vulnerability to an expanding but unstable economy. This apparent division between public and private worlds was nevertheless a misleading one: women's family roles were an integral part of the business enterprise in this period. The new assumptions were important, however, not only within these middle-class ranks but also among the shapers of opinion. As we shall see, the debate about the lives of working-class women from the 1830s was to be profoundly influenced by these middle-class values. The reality of the domestic lives of both working-class and middle-class women have been overshadowed by such debates: we shall look at the labour of the household − cooking, cleaning, washing − and at changing attitudes to motherhood in chapter 4.

# 3

## *Women's Paid Employment 1830–1880*

For the period from 1851 to 1881 we have slightly more reliable indicators of women's paid employment, in the censuses, based on individual occupations, taken every ten years. These are very helpful in suggesting to us the broad outlines of women's paid work by the mid-Victorian period, and a summary is reprinted here: see table 3.1. It will be noted that the largest single category of paid workers is very clearly that of domestic service, which was growing throughout these years. Factory work too has now become an important area of work for some women. The next largest group — though comprising less than half the number of domestic servants — is that of textile workers, closely followed by those in the clothing trades, most in workshops or in outwork. These three groups make up 80 per cent of all women in recorded occupations in 1851. In contrast, the number of women recorded in agricultural work is halved in the years between 1851 and 1881. There is, however, a new and expanding category of professional oc-cupations and subordinate offices. Most other occupational groups employ few women, though at a regional level there are still significant numbers in the metal trades, in food and drink manufacture and also in printing and stationery work.

While these indicators are helpful, they nevertheless have considerable weaknesses. They seriously underrecord the number of employed women, possibly by as much as a third.

TABLE 3.1  Main occupations of females of all ages in Great Britain in 1851 and 1881 (in thousands)

| Occupation | 1851 | 1881 |
| --- | --- | --- |
| Agriculture, horticulture and forestry | 229 | 116 |
| Textiles | 635 | 745 |
| Metal manufacture, machines, implements, vehicles, precious metals, etc. | 36 | 49 |
| Building and construction | 1 | 2 |
| Transport and communications | 13 | 15 |
| Clothing | 491 | 667 |
| Mining, quarrying and workers in the products of mines and quarries | 11 | 8 |
| Food, drink and tobacco | 53 | 98 |
| Domestic offices and personal services | 1,135 | 1,756 |
| Professional occupations and their subordinate services | 103 | 203 |
| Wood, furniture fittings and decorations | 8 | 21 |
| Commercial occupations | − | 11 |
| Bricks, cement, pottery, glass | 15 | 27 |
| Public administration | 3 | 9 |
| Paper, printing, books, stationery | 16 | 53 |
| Chemicals, oil, soap, resin | 4 | 9 |
| Total occupied | 2,832 | 3,887 |
| (Total occupied males) | 6,545 | 8,852 |

*Source*: Angela John (ed.), *Unequal Opportunities: Women's Employment in England 1800–1918* (Oxford: Basil Blackwell, 1985), p. 37.

There is considerable evidence that part-time seasonal and irregular work of all kinds — including seasonal agricultural work, outwork, casual domestic work such as washing, and working in family businesses — were all ignored. Such activities were not necessarily perceived either by women themselves or by others as an 'occupation'. An 'occupation' was generally perceived as the work performed by a male head of household or a single unmarried person. Moreover, certain categories of employment were still recorded inconsistently. The instructions given to householders and enumerators were unclear, particularly in dealing with the work of women within the household or family economy. Many of those recorded as domestic servants were wives, daughters or other relatives of the head of the household. And under the category of domestic servant were also recorded many, whether relatives or not, working in shopkeeping or farming families, whose work might not be expected to be purely domestic.

In this chapter we shall discuss the major categories of employment excluding domestic service, which will be considered in the next chapter. What may be seen in this period is not a wholesale move into factory work by women, though this was important in certain areas. Rather we should see a consolidation, and sometimes a redrawing, of divisions of labour between men and women, sometimes in new settings. But the old overlap and interaction betweem the home and the workplace continued for women though generally not for men — most notably in the sweated trades. Their status as unskilled or at most semi-skilled workers was more clearly defined. And the patterns of authority derived from family relationships undoubtedly shifted into new workplaces.

The history of women's work in this period is very different from that of men's work. This was a period in which a second phase of industrialization brought with it the expansion of heavy industries: iron and steel, shipbuilding, transport, stimulated of course by railway growth, and chemicals. These industries did not provide work for women; but they did contribute considerably to new areas of employment for men, especially skilled craftsmen. By the end of the period, skilled male workers had begun to build a trade-union movement. The Trades Union Congress first met in 1868, representing the interests primarily of the skilled crafts. In this kind of movement women had virtually no place; moreover, one powerful thrust of their campaign was towards the breadwinner's wage for male workers. The assumption that the male worker should aim to support his wife and family was beginning to undermine, in aspiration if not in practice, the older pattern of the family economy to which all members contributed.

From the mid-1820s the mechanization of weaving for the first time brought women in large numbers into textile factories. They had already entered such factories earlier as a minority of spinners and to work on various important mechanized preparatory processes. There could of course be several processes at work in a shift to factory production. This shift might simply concentrate machinery, especially larger machinery, under one roof: more importantly it could entail the application of steam power to the new machinery, to maximize production. The successful application of steam power to the powerloom from 1822 meant that cotton weaving was the first to be mechanized. Others followed: worsted after 1835, wool after 1850 and silk, though to a limited extent only, from the 1820s. In the lace industry, steam power came to be applied to the bobbin-net machine in lace factories from the 1830s. In hosiery, steam power was applied to knitting machinery only from the 1850s and to the women's work of seaming and finishing only from the 1870s. The timing of the entry by women into factory production, even in the textile trades, varied greatly; and for much of this period such factory production coexisted with the survival and sometimes the expansion of domestic industry in these trades. In silk, lacemaking and hosiery, married women in particular continued to work in processes that were still put out to women working at home.

The character of the female labour force in these industries was therefore at any single time quite diverse — but it remained influenced by the assumptions of the family economy. The tasks performed by women were different from those of men: defined as of less skill, and poorly paid. The major exception to this was powerloom weaving in the cotton industry, which from the 1840s was also done by men. There could also be differences — though the contrast was never clearcut — between the work of married and of young single women. In the Lancashire cotton factories, broadly, the majority of those employed were young single women, with a minority of poorer married women. They worked as powerloom weavers or in other preparatory work such as carding. One study, which analysed the census returns of 1851 for seven districts of Lancashire, suggested that overall only 27 per cent of women cotton operatives were either married or widowed. There is some consistent evidence, however, to suggest that from the 1850s to the 1870s the proportion of married and widowed women in the cotton industry was increasing; so in the Blackburn district it went up from 25 to 35 per cent of the total women cotton operatives.

The married woman factory worker was the target of much condemnation from observers of the factory system: but the mothers of small children were probably a small proportion of the overall factory workforce. In the same seven districts of Lancashire of 1851, only one-fifth of those married women in work had children under one year in age, though these numbers were gradually increasing. A family's prosperity depended on how many members were actively contributing to its overall income — and the low point of such an economy was likely to come soon after marriage, when children were too young to contribute anything. The married women who worked in these factory occupations tended to be those whose husbands were poorly paid or out of work. A married woman, if in factory work, was most likely to leave employment in her thirties, when her first children were old enough to enter employment. In one of the few detailed studies of a female factory labour force, that of the Courtaulds' mill in Halstead, Essex, where 90 per cent of workers in the 1860s were women, Judy Lown has shown from the 1861 census that a similar proportion of the women workers, 31 per cent, were married or widowed. Where alternatives existed, married women were more likely to do work which could be done at home. Where there were no such alternatives, and a wife's contribution was needed, she would enter factory employment.

By the 1830s and 1840s the condition of both children and women working in factories had become a subject of public concern. The campaigners of the Ten Hours movement had called for the appallingly long hours worked by children, and by implication by the rest of the family, to be limited by law to ten hours a day. Social and political reformers of all shades, novelists and humanitarians, were to focus for the next two decades on the contrast between their own family lives and the conditions encountered in northern working-class districts. Many such works remain invaluable sources, the products of genuine humanitarian feeling; but it must be remembered that they were filtered through an understanding of family relations very different from those they observed. So, for instance, two key studies, Dr Gaskell's *The Manufacturing Population of England* (1833) and Friedrich Engels, *Condition of the Working Classes in England in 1844* (1845) focused a little sensationally on the absence of working wives from desolate homes, and the inability of working-class men to support their wives. Elizabeth Gaskell wrote two novels set in Manchester, *Mary Barton* (1848) and *North and South* (1854), but neither contained a sympathetic portrait of a woman factory worker: rather, she lamented the higher wages, sense of independence and lack of training in household skills that seemed to characterize the young factory woman.

These views were a part of a continuing debate. Middle-class men and women saw the life of factory workers in the light of their own sense of the appropriate separation of spheres. Working-class men tried to support and defend their family members, often in quite inhumane conditions, and they hoped, by participating in the Ten Hours movement, to secure a reduction in working hours for all. They were also concerned to defend the situation of adult male workers, a small minority within the textile factories, fearing the competition of the cheaper work of women and children if mechanization should go further. So one of the few early male trade unions within the factories, John Docherty's cotton spinners' union, explicitly excluded women workers from 1829; when they were admitted, as some were to branches of local spinners' unions in the 1830s, they were organized in separate sections as piecers or cardroom operatives. The protective legislation of the 1830s and 1840s came from these different perspectives. Unfortunately we do not know how far women workers themselves welcomed this legislation, which could threaten to reduce their earnings.

The Factory Act of 1833, applicable to all textile factories except the silk mills, limited the hours of young people under eighteen to twelve hours a day and prohibited night work for them, and excluded children under nine from the mills. The first legislation to protect women workers separately came with the Mines Act of 1842, a response to the report on the appalling underground conditions in which women and children worked. Although the report had originally been intended to deal with children only, the revelations it contained so shocked the reading public and the parliamentarians that women were completely prohibited from underground work in mines. That act was followed by the Factory Act of 1844, which for the first time excluded women from night work and limited their hours also to twelve a day; and by later acts which were intended to provide a uniform working day for women, young people and children. Legislation did not of course necessarily imply enforcement. These acts did include provision for a new Factory Inspectorate, though its numbers and powers were extremely limited in the early years.

The implications of this legislation are interesting. It was not applicable to adult male workers, though the long-term effect was to create a more clearly defined uniform working day for all in the industries affected. For the first time, therefore, women workers, like children, were seen as a special category requiring protection. Yet the application of the law was extremely selective. With the exception, arguably, of coal-mining, the work protected in this way was not necessarily the heaviest, or the conditions the worst, of the work done by women. The heavy labour of the domestic servant or the washerwoman was never addressed in such legislation. Slowly the protection of women workers in other industries – pottery, glass, paper, tobacco – was extended in legislation from the 1850s to the 1890s. The Workshop Act of 1867 defined its application as to any establishment employing more than fifty workers. But no enquiry was made into the exploitation of the sweated trades until the first decade of the twentieth century.

This legislation broadly reflected the views both of social reformers and of most male trade unionists. Approaching the issue from different directions, both were opposed to the extension of women's work, especially where it might conflict with the interests of male workers. Both shared the view that an adult male worker should be able to support his wife and children from his own earnings. There were of course some variations in the attitudes of male workers: where both husband and wife were by custom engaged in the same kind of work — for instance, cotton weaving — such work continued to be seen as necessary to the family income. And as has been seen in the exchange between Lord Manners and Richard Muggeridge quoted above (see Introduction), domestic industry might be appropriate where factory work was not. Clearly many women too shared this view. Jane Humphries has argued that to concentrate on maximizing the 'breadwinner's wage' was a defensible and rational strategy for all members of the family by the 1840s (Humphries, 1981). But it has also been suggested that for some male workers economic necessity might prevail over principle. And some coal miners, working in areas still governed by the family economy, opposed the exclusion of women from the pits (John, 1980, p. 59). The problem remains a complex one, but it is still true that the older assumptions of the family economy were gradually being undercut by the emergence of the 'breadwinner's wage'. Middle-class models contributed to such a theme, but it arose more fundamentally from the situation of male workers in an industrializing society. At the Trades Union Congress in 1877 Henry Broadhurst, as president, supported restrictions on women's work in terms which echo the notion of separate spheres:

It was their duty as men and husbands to use their utmost efforts to bring about a condition of things where their wives should be in their proper sphere at home, seeing after their house and family, instead of being dragged into the competition for livelihood against the great and strong men of the world. (Quoted in Bornat, 1985, p. 209)

It remained true, however, that the majority of working-class men, in this period and long after, did not receive such a 'breadwinner's wage'.

The conditions of women's work, then, were not determined simply by economic factors – the demand for their labour – but by a complex mixture of attitudes, shared by employers and by male workers, which related women's lives at work to their family roles. Feminist historians have called attention to the patriarchal structures of women's working lives as well as their family lives. By this is meant the maintenance of authority of men over women, in the workplace as well as in the home. The conflict between economic and patriarchal motives has been traced, for instance, in the cotton industry, in the search for and introduction of the 'self-acting mule', a mule-spinning machine which could be operated by women without the need for skilled male workers, who were both more expensive and better organized. These machines were introduced into factories in the 1830s and 1840s: but it has been pointed out that although the nature of the work did change, the old supervisory structure was retained (Lazonick, 1979). The skilled male mule-spinner was replaced by the less skilled but still male minder, whose task in particular was to supervise the piecers and scavengers, boys, girls and women. Employers chose, for a variety of reasons, to perpetuate this gender division: one of these reasons was undoubtedly the view that overseeing and supervisory tasks should remain in the hands of, and were most effectively performed by, men.

Such structures have similarly been analysed by Judy Lown in her work on the Courtaulds' Halstead factory in Essex. There in 1861 in a largely female workforce, out of a total of 901 women workers of whom 589 were weavers, only four women occupied positions of authority as female assistant overseers, their task to assist male overseers in the winding sheds where young children worked. The female workforce was supervised by a manager and twenty-six male overseers, out of a total of 114 male workers. Only a small number of male workers were recruited; but those who were might expect to work their way up the ladder to the skilled and better-paid positions of overseers and clerks. Women could not expect such promotion. Even within a factory dependent on women's work, employers could associate the factory with an ideal of family life, through exercising a form of paternalism in the workplace. That paternalism rested on a sense of appropriate gender divisions. So, in the discipline of the mill, women were more likely to suffer punishment for 'immoral behaviour' and unsuitable dress, men for drunkenness. By the 1850s the Courtaulds employed a woman welfare officer, set up an infant nursery, initiated Maternal Meetings and an evening school and set up a Factory Home for working girls. These initiatives were not necessarily welcomed, but their aim was undoubtedly to carry a message of domesticity to working women, however paradoxical that might appear. The ideal of paternalism was clearly important also in the factories of Lancashire, but we lack any similar analysis of its effects.

By the late nineteenth century, sections of the female factory labour force were undoubtedly among the better-paid women workers. There were also signs of their organization in the textile industries. In 1875 a group of Dewsbury women, working in the woollen industry, formed what was to be the first branch of the General Union of Textile Workers, first called the Dewsbury, Batley and Heavy Woollen District Woollen Weavers Association, in defending women workers against a wage cut by manufacturers. Though at first the union consisted mainly of women, it came to be dominated by men. In the 1880s and 1890s women were gradually to appear in new unions of this kind formed in Lancashire and Yorkshire: some women were to achieve prominence, though the leadership always lay with men. Women's work, by now clearly defined and differentiated from that of men, was to continue to be a contentious and divisive issue for women and men in the emergent labour movement.


WOMEN'S TRADES AND THE GROWTH OF THE
SWEATED TRADES

The tendency for women working in urban trades to see their condition deteriorating by the early nineteenth century continued. The drive towards increasing mass production, which might be accompanied by mechanization, forced male skilled craftsmen to defend their position as their livelihood was threatened: the outcome for most women workers in these trades could only be exclusion from skilled work and employment in subdivided and unskilled work. There were, of course, some exceptions to this. In the London trades, women might at mid-century be employed as journeywomen, serving some sort of apprenticeship (in the hatting or bookbinding trades, for example), but their work was still carefully defined as different to that of men. Elsewhere there were few opportunities left for girls to become apprentices except in dressmaking, millinery and mantua making. In small establishments, these were largely female trades, though even those catering to a fashionable clientele and employing skilled women required very long hours of work and offered low pay. This did, however, represent one area where it was possible, given great good fortune, to become a successful businesswoman. Margaret Oliphant's heroine in her novel *Kirsteen* (1888), having rejected marriage, unusually did just that. In less appropriate trades, by the late nineteenth century it would appear to have been very difficult for women to run a successful business, though little research exists on this subject.

In the printing industry, women were effectively excluded by male workers during this period. There were important new technological developments: the steam press was introduced in 1814, stereotyping (taking a mould of sections of type for mass production) in the 1830s, new composing machinery in the 1850s. Equally important was the enormous expansion of business in the first half of the century. Male unions – the provincial Typographical Association and the London Society of Compositors – both attempted to reserve the new compositing machinery for men only, arguing that women were both unsuitable and incompetent for the job. They aimed to protect their own wages from the competition of women, who from 1860 were taken on by some provincial employers and paid notably less. The London Society deplored these low rates but still refused to admit women to its ranks so that they might receive the union rate. Their defence was largely successful, confirmed with the emergence by the late 1880s of the linotype machine which made type-distribution again a skilled — and therefore by implication masculine — task. The printers remained in a powerful position in their trade until very recently.

By contrast, women bookbinders preserved their skill and status, though also their low wages relative to skilled men, until mechanization in the 1880s changed the pattern of labour. Machines were then introduced to cover most of the processes involved, and women were no longer confined to folding and sewing but were likely to be directed towards operating what was seen as simple machinery in a range of unskilled tasks. But a unionized male workforce, though a minority of an industry in which women had a long-standing place, was able to retain its control over higher paid, skilled work, to which women were no longer admitted. In both industries the existence of strong male organization before a late mechanization allowed them to protect their position, in a particularly marked confrontation between men and women workers. The small group of skilled women in such trades had no such weapons.

In examining the expansion of domestic industry in the eighteenth century, we noted that this was often the most profitable course available to entrepreneurs because of the availability of the cheap labour of women and children at home. Throughout the nineteenth century, putting work out to women workers either at home or in small workshops could still remain the preferred course in certain industries. Again this might be particularly true where women had no alternative employment, particularly in the countryside. New technology introduced in factories could bring more work to be put out; and one of the most important technical innovations for women's work in this period, the sewing machine, might be seen as one which encouraged outwork.

In the silk industry in Coventry, domestic weavers attempted in the 1850s to compete with the factories by harnessing steam power to their own home-based systems, providing power to a group of families in a row or group of houses, though after the

1860s in a declining industry they could no longer compete. In the framework-knitting industry by the 1850s, women in Leicester were mainly working as seamers, though in the rural districts of Leicestershire 40 per cent of the knitting frames were operated by women. After 1870 the invention of a machine which could perform the women's work of seaming took that task too into the factories, though again it employed women there. Nancy Grey Osterud has noted that a similar division of labour between men and women was extended into the boot and shoe industry when that expanded in Leicester after the mid-century. Women did the stitching of the uppers in their homes, with hand-operated machines rented to them by entrepreneurs. Men did all other tasks within the factories. Entrepreneurs chose to follow the customary pattern of work in the town.

In the lacemaking industry of Nottingham, as we have seen, outwork survived and expanded for much of this period. Although the making of the nets was now in factories, all the final processes of mending, 'running' and embroidering the nets were done by hand and involved much hand-done needlework by women and by children. One witness, a Mrs Barber who employed her own family, gave evidence to the Royal Commission on Children's Employment in 1843 that:

> There are in Nottingham from 80 to 100 mistresses who take lace to embroider; these mistresses employ young women at their own houses, and on an average about five to ten each; they also employ a number of women at Nottingham, Leicester, Derby, Sutton and the neighbouring villages; the women to whom the work is thus given employ themselves, children, and young persons, and again deliver out a part of the lace to other parties, so that sometimes the work goes through three and occasionally four hands ... (Quoted in Bythell, 1978, p. 100)

Such systems did see a decline with the new educational legislation of the 1870s which made school compulsory for young children, but it remained perfectly viable for women until the end of the century. In other rural areas, for instance Devonshire, women continued to make pillow-lace by hand in significant numbers until at least the 1860s.

In some ways the history of women's work in the metal trades of the West Midlands comes to share the same characteristics: within the industry, men are more likely to enter factory production, women to remain at work in the smaller rural workshops and homes. The long-established hand nail-making industry from the 1830s was facing both foreign and factory competition: in decline the trade came to be seen as providing a supplementary branch of the family income and to rely more on women workers, with a consequent depression in wages. Its location shifted from the Black Country north of Birmingham to the more remote and semi-agricultural countryside around Bromsgrove. The decline accelerated from the 1870s. Chainmaking, on the other hand, was an expanding trade from the 1820s, focused almost entirely on Cradley. In this trade too the homeworkers were mainly women, the factory workers exclusively men. The largest and heaviest chains were made within factories: and even in outwork there was a division between men's and women's work – the lightest and smallest chains were made by women. This outwork industry though growing suffered from short-term fluctuations; and women workers formed an increasing part of the labour force from the 1870s to the beginning of the twentieth century.

But the best-known and most notorious kind of outwork performed by women in this period was in the clothing trades. As we saw in looking at the early nineteenth century, the growing demand for cheap readymade mass-produced clothing – especially men's clothing – created a substantial new industry whose needs could not be met by the craft of tailoring. The process of subdividing the work into different stages, and putting these different stages out to workers in their homes, continued to expand steadily; and by the 1830s in London the tailors had lost control of the readymade trade, though they retained what was called the 'bespoke' or individual and luxury trade. The condition of needlewomen in London in the 1840s was notoriously poor: Henry Mayhew wrote in 1849 of the hours they worked for the most pitifully small sums, far from a living wage:

> I had seen so much want since I began my investigation into the condition of the labouring poor in London that my feelings were almost blunted to sights of ordinary misery. Still I was unprepared for the amount of misery that I have lately witnessed. I could not have believed that there were human beings toiling so long and gaining so little, and starving so silently and heroically, round about our very homes. (Quoted in Bythell, 1978, p. 80)

Philanthropists observed that this was one of the occupational groups from which women might out of absolute need practise casual prostitution.

The structure of work had come to depend on a subcontracting system, with tailors and journeymen becoming subcontractors for employers. Factories where machinery might aid particular operations, the small workshops of subcontractors, and the putting out of particular processes to women, coexisted in the trade. The key was subdivision of the work involved: cutting out and machining were the processes most commonly done centrally, but needlework, pressing and finishing were more likely to go out to workers. Not only in London but in all the major urban centres − Leeds, Manchester, Liverpool, Birmingham and elsewhere − there were major clothing industries with a proportion of the work being put out to women in rural districts, sometimes by rail.

The development of the trade varied from city to city. The sewing machine, marketed from 1851, tended to increase the volume of handwork that could be done. Power-driven machinery was also used by some larger employers from the 1850s. The Leeds clothing trade was among the most advanced in its organization, as subdivision of work had gone further and the work was done in larger workshops than in London. But as in London the characteristic feature of the trade, wherever the work was done, was the increasing dilution of skill, and the increasing employment of women and girls at extremely low rates of pay. This was what constituted the 'sweated' trades; and the numbers employed continued to grow steadily in the last quarter of the nineteenth century. In London in 1891 women made up 59 per cent of the workforce in the clothing trades, and in Leeds 70 per cent: the Leeds model was to be that of the future.

The women workers discussed in this section, poorly paid, many of them homeworkers and vulnerable to shifts in trade, clearly were not easy to organize. There were occasional spontaneous strike movements. In 1840 the lace runners at Nottingham formed an association and organized a 'turn-out' against the numbers of those involved – often two or three between contractor and embroideress – in putting work out and therefore taking profits in the industry. Their circular 'To the Lace-runners of Nottingham and its vicinity' read:

> Sisters,
> ... Are you thus to be robbed of your hard-earned pittance to maintain these cormorants in idleness and many of their husbands in drunkenness and profligacy; – no wonder that misery enters our dwellings – that we are in the depth of poverty, that our children are crying for bread, while there is a swarm of locusts hovering between us and the manufacturers ready to devour one half of our hire, it is not enough that we have to compete with machines which, in many cases, supersedes needlework: but are also robbed in the manner described above ...
> (Quoted in Pinchbeck, 1981, p. 213).

Occasionally there could be cooperation between men and women workers. In the 1830s and 1840s journeymen bookbinders in London and Westminster petitioned employers on behalf of women workers who 'often have not the power to plead their own cause in such matters' and were in fact excluded from the Bookbinders Union. In 1867 women outworkers supported a strike of journeymen tailors in the London bespoke trade and received strike pay from their union. But there is no evidence of any union organization among women in the sweated clothing trades in the period before 1880. In 1874 Emma Paterson, of middle-class background but a former bookbinder, founded the Women's Protective and Provident League, whose aims were to act as a central body as well as a benefit society, and to foster the establishment of individual unions. Paterson's ideas were a mixture of feminism, trade unionism and philanthropy. She was profoundly aware of the weakness of women workers and their difficulties of organization, and did encourage a number of small societies, in bookbinding, millinery and skilled sewing trades. Through this organization, women delegates attended the TUC for the first time in 1875, though they were to face long and difficult battles there.

## NEW JOBS FOR WOMEN

One of the growing sections of employment for women is that termed 'professional'. Today it is one of the largest single categories of employment for women; but in the censuses from 1851 to 1881 that category had a rather different meaning. Although the numbers of women involved were small, it is important to notice this group. They represent the small beginnings of that non-domestic 'service sector' of the economy in which today two-thirds of employed women are to be found.

The new jobs for women were to have some clear characteristics. They were to be posts which fitted the middle-class Victorian conception of womanhood. The work was to be clean, light, respectable, carried out mainly among other women: heavy physical work and the moral dangers of mixing with large numbers of men were both excluded. In addition, such work called for a reasonable level of education, in a society where educational standards were changing fast and a high level of female illiteracy was no longer acceptable. Finally, given the expansion of the economy these jobs met growing demands − for a higher level of education and health, for office work for private companies and the government, and for retailing. Much of this demand was only beginning to be heard by 1880. These kind of jobs might appeal to young women from the middle classes and from the upper working class; they were much more likely to be done by single unmarried women than by the married.

Perhaps the best-known of such jobs in this period was that of the governess who figures so largely in mid-nineteenth-century novels, just because this was the most obvious recourse for young middle-class women who needed to support themselves. But the figure of the governess is a well-known one also because of the contemporary concern expressed about her employment. The number of governesses on the market was seen to depress their wages. And it was clear by the 1820s that governesses were quite inadequately qualified for their jobs. Few girls' schools could offer an effective education, most running simply as small private extended family establishments, congenial places for girls to spend two or three years. By 1844 as a result of these discussions a new college for girls, Queen's College, had been set up, soon to be followed by Bedford College. Both were secondary schools rather than offering any equivalent of higher education. The question of the education of middle-class girls had for the first time been opened up, though the numbers tutored in these early establishments were small. Being a governess, or opening a small, private school, remained an important resource for middle-class or lower-middle-class women in this period, though new developments pointed to a different kind of future in education.

Among those campaigning for the improved education of middle-class girls were leading feminists. Emily Davies succeeded in getting the university local examinations of Oxford and Cambridge (broadly the equivalent of GCSE and Advanced Level examinations) thrown open to girls from 1863. Moreover, a range of new types of schools for middle-class girls were founded over the next twenty years. The Taunton Commission set up by the government in 1864 to look at endowed schools, such as the long-established boys' grammar schools, was persuaded to look at girls' education too, and to allow the new Endowed Schools Commission to transfer funds to provide more endowed schools for girls. In 1869 there were only twelve such schools, but 1895 there were eighty. Another way in which middle-class fathers committed themselves to improved education for their daughters could be through the Girls' Public Day School Trust, founded in 1872, which sold shares to secure capital, to set up good day schools of a high academic standard. Finally, following the movement to establish new boys' public schools for the middle classes, a number of new boarding schools for girls were founded — Cheltenham Ladies' College, Roedean, Benenden.

The way was opened therefore for young middle-class women both to secure a better education and perhaps to utilize it in the teaching profession at a high level. Admission to universities was secured only in the final decade of our period. Girton College was founded by Emily Davies in 1869, though women were only admitted to the tripos in 1881. The first Oxford women's college, Lady Margaret Hall, opened in 1879; and other colleges followed. In neither Oxford nor Cambridge were women admitted to full membership until 1919 and 1947 respectively. The University of London, however, opened its examinations and degrees on equal terms in 1878, and provincial universities were gradually to follow. These provisions, however, affected only a very small number of women. Parental opposition to higher education or a teaching career for young middle-class women remained extremely strong.

What did affect significant numbers of women from different classes was the possibility of elementary-school teaching in a rapidly growing educational system. It was on this changing system that all 'new jobs' rested. For most of this period the literacy rates of women were significantly lower than those of men, though our major measure of literacy is a very rough one: the ability to sign the marriage register. One historian has estimated that in the 1780s an average of 68 per cent of men but only 39 per cent of women could sign the marriage register (Laqueur, 1974). The early stages of industrialization brought a fall in literacy in the most affected regions: one suggestion is that in Manchester, for instance, female literacy may have fallen from around 29 per cent in the 1750s to only 19 per cent for 1810–20. But in unaffected areas and after the 1830s, women were gradually narrowing the gap. By 1844 the national literacy figures (again based on marriage registers) were 63 per cent and 52 per cent for men and women, though there were very wide regional variations (Porter, 1843 section V, pp. 278–81; Sanderson, 1983, pp. 10–16).

The eighteenth-century provision for girls' elementary education offered a variety of small 'dame' schools, private schools and charitable, Sunday, or industrial schools. Two voluntary societies, the National Society for Promoting the Education of the Poor in the Church of England, and the British and Foreign Schools Society, backed by Nonconformists, founded in 1811 and 1814 respectively, gradually created networks of schools which were eventually given aid and supervised by the state from the 1830s. Legislation in 1870 and 1876 was to bring these schools under state control and to make elementary education both free and compulsory. Though this was not immediately achieved, it was in the next two decades to eliminate the literacy differentials between women and men. State responsibility for secondary education, however, was not finally assumed until 1902.

The voluntary societies were concerned about the educational standards of their teachers, and from 1812 set up small training departments for teachers attached to schools. So too did the new movement for infant education. The most successful of these early training colleges was the Home and Colonial Training College, founded in London in 1836 by the Home and Colonial Infant School Society, which in its first ten years trained 1443 teachers, mainly single women. As the state extended its supervision over the voluntary societies in 1839, a network of training colleges was established between 1839 and 1864. Fees were charged at around £20 a year and the length of courses varied from three months to three years. In 1846 a new scheme for pupil-teachers offered those who could pass an examination a subsidy of the cost of four-fifths of their training. This system offered young women in effect a new kind of apprenticeship — a period from the ages of thirteen to eighteen as a pupil-teacher, rewarded for success by further

74

training. Between 1849 and 1859 the number of pupil-teachers at work in schools rose from 3,580 to 15,224, and the proportion of girls from 32 to 46 per cent.

The pupil-teacher scheme was directed towards bright working-class girls. Yet a detailed study of one early college opened in 1841, Whitelands in Putney, shows some variations (Widdowson, 1980). The entrants initially came from very diverse backgrounds, including ex-domestic servants, the daughters of artisans, clerks and the lower middle classes, together with girls from professional families. To begin with there was no age limit, since women might come in their mid-twenties. In 1851 some 10 per cent of girls at Whitelands were from a professional background, just over 50 per cent from the lower middle classes and the rest working-class. By 1881 the proportion of working-class girls was 41 per cent, those from the lower middle classes 53 per cent, and girls from professional families only 6 per cent. Life at the college was hard, with a spartan lifestyle and strenuous domestic duties, unlikely to appeal to many who thought of themselves as 'ladies'.

By 1875 women represented just over half of all elementary-school teachers and the proportion was to continue to rise, until by 1914 three-quarters were women. However, not all of these − in fact only 57 per cent − were trained and certified. There were other routes by which women might be employed: by taking 'acting teachers' examinations', or being approved by a government inspector. The 1881 census records 122,846 women as employed in teaching, though it does not separate the different categories of teachers. This, however, was clearly an important area of work − primarily for unmarried women − requiring both training and qualifications, but also perceived as suitable for women, especially at the lower levels. In many ways it represents a further consolidation of the sexual division of labour.

So too do other examples of this category. Nursing, for instance, is recorded in the census of 1851 not as a professional occupation but as a form of domestic service. Though this was to change, it reflects one contemporary perspective on this work. There was of course a significant group of nurses, including sisters and matrons of some responsibility, employed in voluntary and workhouse hospitals, and in private homes, before Florence Nightingale began her work. Some came from the lower middle classes, others had been previously in service. The image of them that has remained is of the drunken and incompetent: this probably seriously maligns many nurses, yet we have little reliable information on this. From the 1840s onwards the need to transform nursing into a new kind of occupation was inspired by a sense of its appropriateness for women, by religious commitment and by a drive toward a medical reform. The pioneers were members of religious orders, including not only that at Kaiserswerth in Germany admired by Florence Nightingale, but new Anglican orders, the Sisters of Mercy founded in 1845 and St John's House in 1848.

The problems for the new profession were to spring from these contradictory origins. Of all these 'new jobs' nursing perhaps most embodies the contradictions between the expect-ations of women, in terms of both gender and class, and the nature of the work involved. Were nurses to be comparable to domestic servants, or reforming angels? Most practically, were they to be working-class women, or ladies? The problems bedevilled Florence Nightingale's party in the Crimea, where the lady volunteers expected to be waited on by the working-class women who had come as nurses. Even Nightingale her-self first anticipated that recruits to her Nightingale School founded at St Thomas in 1860 would be working women: realizing the need for future sisters and matrons, she then introduced a class of special 'lady pupils'. Gradually, however, these distinctions disappeared. The range of nursing special-izations increased — workhouse nursing, district nursing, private nursing and nursing for the armed services. The oldest form, midwifery, however, had to wait until 1902 for recognition and a form of registration. By 1881, 35,175 women were recorded as nurses, though this figure included members of religious orders and casual or untrained nurses. This almost entirely female profession grew over the next decades.

Other 'new jobs' were less important numerically, though in

the future they were to be much more so. The capitalist society of mid-Victorian England, producing, consuming, selling, needed a substantial service sector. Young educated women could provide the workforce needed for the shops and offices of this society, though for them to do so, public attitudes had to shift, and male opposition be overcome. In the later nineteenth century the mid-Victorian shop run by the independent shopkeeper, with perhaps a few male apprentices, was to give way at least in the larger cities to the department store; and the decline of the old tradition brought a replacement of skilled by unskilled workers. However, women shop assistants would be introduced not into the heavier trades or those serving a male clientele, but where no great training was needed and customers were mainly women: in shops selling drapery, millinery, underwear, food, flowers or stationery and other goods. We have no reliable figures on the employment of shop assistants, but some contemporaries saw the dramatic increase in the employment of women as taking place from the 1870s.

The same process at the end of the period was to see a considerable growth in the numbers of women office-workers. The mid-Victorian office had drawn clerks and apprentices from boys of the middle classes. The expansion of business concerns and the demand for clerical labour involved brought a ready demand for the cheaper work of women, sometimes better educated than the men they replaced. And the coming of the typewriter − widely sold from 1882 − confirmed this: the skills of typing were frequently compared to those of pianoplaying. Even before women entered private offices in significant numbers they had been found valuable in the service of government and in particular in the Post Office. In the mid-1850s private telegraph companies had found women employees to be 'more teachable, more attentive and quicker eyed ... also more trustworthy, more easily managed and ... sooner satisfied with lower wages' (Holcombe, 1973, p. 165) than the men previously employed. When these companies were taken over by the Post Office in 1870, women continued to be employed. Almost as soon as telephones were made available in 1879, women became telephone operators. The first government department to employ women as clerks was also the Post Office, and from there they spread to other departments. They worked strictly segregated from the male clerks. Women were not employed in the higher grades of the civil service, except for a very small number of women inspectors of areas seen as appropriate for women, such as workhouse schools and infirmaries, educational establishments, especially those dealing with domestic subjects, and factories where large numbers of women were employed. By 1881, 53,106 women were employed directly by the central government (compared to a total of only 6,420 women clerks known to be privately employed). The signs of future expansion were clear.

Mid-nineteenth-century feminists were deeply concerned with women's employment; but it is paradoxical that though they wished it to be both recognized and extended, their arguments were for the admission of women to occupations for which they were particularly fitted, for the service jobs which fell so naturally into women's 'sphere'. Industrialization for women did not bring an expansion of women's opportunities in manufacturing industry. Rather, with an increasingly clear-cut definition of gender roles, it enabled some women's labour to be cheaply used, while for others it brought occupations which might be seen as reflecting the concerns of their domestic lives. It is finally to the transformation of women's domestic lives in a century of economic change that we need to turn.

# 4

## *Domestic Life and Labour*

What characterized the lives of middle-class women in an age
of industrialization was not their employment but the forms of
domesticity adopted, which were integrally related to the
economic changes of that age. The new focus on the home
reflected the importance of the consuming household rather
than the producing one — for the middle-class home was a
prime consumer of the new products of the industrial revolution.
Historians have not yet adequately discussed the relationship
between ideals of domesticity and the material reality of the
Victorian household, whether middle-class or working-class.
How far could middle-class women in practice retreat from the
labour of that household? It has been argued that the ideology
of domesticity sketched in chapter 2 permeated downwards
into working-class homes through the dominance of the opinion-
shaping middle classes. It has also been suggested that when,
after labouring in middle-class houses, domestic servants married
and set up their own households, they carried into them the
same domestic outlook. These arguments have to be set against
what we know of domestic life and work in Victorian England.

In the fifty years after 1830, legal changes in marriage did
come to reflect the themes which dominated educated opinion:
the need for a secular and nationally regulated approach to
marriage, and much clearer and up-to-date law on the relationship between husband and wife. So the Births, Marriages,

and Deaths Act of 1837, passed partly to meet the wishes of Nonconformists, had the effect of setting up a simple secular civil procedure for marriage, cheaper than a church wedding. Gradually older regional customs, and belief in the importance of betrothal, were to give way to the alternatives of a religious wedding or a civil ceremony, both as prescribed by law. Similarly there was much support, for a variety of reasons, for a rationalization of the chaotic legal system regulating marriage. Feminists were to agree with legal reformers on this, in some respects at least. In 1857 divorce was introduced for the first time, the church courts' role abolished, and a new secular court set up to deal with divorce cases. The grounds on which divorce was possible, however, reflected the double standard applied to men and women: women might be divorced for adultery alone, men only if adultery was accompanied by some other offence, such as cruelty, bigamy or desertion. By the end of our period the principle that married women should be able to own their own property had been accepted. In 1870 they won the right to their own earnings, and in 1882 the right to all other forms of property including landed property.

A society whose educated elite was profoundly committed to the ideas of individualism could not tolerate the survival of such a confused and patriarchal legal structure as that sketched in chapter 2. It is ironic that it was the mid-Victorian world – so condemned for its patriarchalism – which began, however tentatively, to dismantle the legal structures of the past. Domesticity had its contradictions: it could symbolize an equal but different partnership, as almost all feminists of the period would have suggested.

But legal changes of this kind, while giving us some idea of the thinking of an elite, can tell us little about the reality of the domestic lives of the majority of the population, for whom in practice there was no access to divorce, and for whom the right to own property was mostly irrelevant. To locate such domestic lives, for both middle- and working-class women, we can look at the housing in which women and men lived, at what is known about the kind of domestic labour needed to maintain families and about the responsibilities of mothers for their children.

Our ideas about Victorian domesticity are largely derived from the advice manuals and prescriptive literature addressed to the Victorian middle classes. There were of course great diversities among them. The great industrialists, bankers and merchants had a lifestyle very different from that of the middling ranks of the professionals and smaller manufacturers. These in their turn differed from the rapidly growing ranks of the lower middle classes, not only shopkeepers and tradesmen but teachers, clerks, bookkeepers. The advice manuals directed to women tell us much about the domestic lifestyles appropriate to each income bracket, and consequently about the proper concerns of the woman married to a clerk or a doctor or a successful industrialist.

But first, their priority was to illustrate the ideal domestic setting, a setting often far removed in the imagination from the realities of economic change. By the 1830s it was clear that the ideal of Victorian womanhood was to be firmly located in the material context of the home. So one of the most influential writers of the 1830s, John Claudius Loudon, amplified and developed the notion of domesticity in his works, of which the best-known were *The Suburban Gardener and Villa Companion* (1838) and *The Encyclopaedia of Cottage, Farm and Villa Architecture and Furniture* (1833). In these he aimed to show how the pleasures of country life might be recreated in the suburban house and garden, for those seeking to separate themselves from the bustle of towns and cities. By implication, the domestic sphere of middle-class women was being separated from the world of economic exchange. In such works as Walsh's *Manual of Domestic Economy: suited to families spending from £100 to £1000 a Year* (1853), suitable households and lifestyles for families living on £100, £250, £500 and £1,000 were described and compared.

The private detached villa, with garden, was of course not available to all members of the middle classes. Most families rented their homes, and could normally spend around a tenth of their annual income on rent. The fine terraced housing which was so marked a feature of late Georgian and Regency building was to give way to the suburban villa, or as a compromise the semi-detached house. Even these might seem unrealizable aspirations for many. Lower-middle-class families on low incomes might well be most likely to live in a superior mid-Victorian terraced house, little different from that of the artisan or tradesman. The suburbs of South London, full of such mid- and late-Victorian terraces, were built for the clerks and white-collar workers commuting to the offices of the city. Whatever form the household took in reality, a continuing theme remained the separation put between the home and a husband's place of work. The domestic household became the private home, no longer for the most part an extension of a trade, shop or business.

This separation of worlds could be paralleled in the different domains, masculine and feminine, within the well-to-do middle-class family, where the study, library and billiard room were masculine preserves, the drawing rooms, sewing and music rooms largely for the ladies. In most middle-class houses, however, it was not possible to reserve more than a study at best for the husband and father: the rest of the house was governed by a code of behaviour regulated by women.

The self-sufficiency of the household was encouraged in the course of the nineteenth century by the provision of services such as water, sanitation and gas directly to middle-class housing. Though some middle-class housing, for instance in London, had piped water from the early nineteenth century or earlier, it was rarely piped beyond the ground floor till the 1860s. Early fixed baths put in from the 1840s had to be filled and emptied by hand. The better middle-class houses were being built with bathrooms by the 1870s, but adoption was still slow. This was true also of sanitation. Many early Victorian homes simply relied on the 'privy' at the end of the garden. Only with new sanitation systems and non-porous piping from the 1850s was rapid progress made, and over the next twenty years middle-class houses were built with integral water-closets. Gas lighting was introduced from the 1840s, though gas was not used extensively for cooking until the 1890s. Such changes came slowly; but the existence of water piped to the individual home meant that the middle-class household was able to set itself new standards in cleanliness and comfort.

This was not the case for the working-class wife and mother. For her, notions of domesticity, privacy and respectability were far removed from her environment. Neither the rural cottage nor the housing of the early industrial revolution offered such possibilities. The rural cottage, usually built of local materials — brick or stone if available, or half-timber, clay and mud — would have only one ground-floor room, and perhaps two small bedrooms, sometimes only one. Windows would be small and scarce, piped water unknown. Families would have to rely on the village pump or well. Such cottages too were scarce, insufficient in number to meet the needs of the growing population, especially as living in on the farm was declining. The pressure for accommodation brought with it overcrowding, decay and squalor in rural cottages and hovels as bad as anything to be found in the industrial towns. Some landowners tried to develop model housing, but their numbers were small. The need for better standards was acknowledged by the 1880s, but change was slow to come, and the conditions of the urban population of this period, however poor by twentieth-century standards, should be seen against this history.

The housing of those attracted to the growing cities, or to the clusters of industrial villages, could take different forms; but most were overcrowded and insanitary. In the central borough of Manchester around 1840 there were probably 15,000–20,000 people living in cellar-dwellings, the basements of other houses. They were likely to have two rooms, little light, and to lack drainage; in Liverpool, too, many families lived in such conditions. In older cities, housing which had once been for the well-to-do might be subdivided and become the tenement homes of many families. But the most common form was that of the terrace or court of small houses, often built back-to-back. Such buildings might be fitted into existing spaces with houses built around small enclosed courts, linked by alleys. In some areas family homes might incorporate areas for domestic industry as late as the 1840s. In Nottingham and the framework-knitting districts a third storey might be built on to terraces for laceworkers or knitters to work in. By mid-century, however, the 'through' terraces, facing the open street rather than enclosed courts or alleys, were coming to be the most usual form of building.

These patterns of housing are very relevant to women's daily lives and domestic work. In the cellars and tenements of the older cities, and in the courts set back from through streets, families might live in one pump to a street or court. Equally, shared and squalid privies could serve numbers of families. Any washing was likely to be done in cooperation and strung across the street or court to dry. Under such circumstances the middle-class ideal of the private, domestic world was a long way away from the labour that went into surviving in such environments.

At the same time, not all working-class families lived in the cellars, tenements and courts of the great industrial cities. Those families in work, especially with a skill or trade, might live in three or four rooms, with some furniture. One report on the homes of the skilled Coventry silk weavers in 1840 described them as 'good, comfortable dwellings; some of them very well furnished; many have nice clocks, and beds and drawers, some ornamented with prints: and some have comfortable parlours' (quoted in Burnett, 1978, p. 56). Some of the new terraced housing built for the skilled artisan by the middle of the nineteenth century equally could promise better things: two bedrooms, with a parlour as well as a kitchen, and perhaps an individual privy, could provide more space and privacy. The front parlour carefully decorated and furnished could symbolize the possibilities of a more domestic and private life.

By the 1880s the conditions of urban life of the 1840s had been condemned by government and local authorities. But improvement was a very lengthy process, and regional differences were great. The adoption of building controls and the Public Health Act of 1875 were gradually to control and regularize the standards of housing, and by the 1890s water was individually piped to working-class houses in many towns, though by no means all.

The overcrowded rural cottage was likely to be more squalid and insanitary than much urban housing by the late nineteenth century. In towns and cities the random growth of the earlier period gave way to patterns of building which were regulated and which undoubtedly gave greater space and better sanitation, though in some areas the older pattern was to continue. The terraced housing of the second half of the nineteenth century still presented a considerable contrast to the semi-detached house or villa which was the middle-class ideal. There a new sense of community or of neighbourhood might emerge from the households of the streets or terraces where women were likely to spend much of their (unpaid) working lives. The particular kind of domestic life which women were likely to experience had as much, or more, to do with the material context of their lives as with any ideology of behaviour.

### THE LABOUR OF HOUSEWORK

Within this period the meaning attached to the word 'housewife' shifts significantly, though we still need much more research on the nature of these shifts. As we have seen, until the early nineteenth century, it was assumed by middle- and working-class men and women that most women would contribute through paid work to the well-being of their families, though also caring for their physical needs. By the later nineteenth century the married working-class woman saw her work as mainly the *unpaid* work of the housewife, though she might well also contribute to the family income in other ways. Daughters learnt their expectations from their mothers and very many would also spend their youth in domestic service. The technology and context of housework changed to some extent during this period. The middle-class household would hope to purchase the products of the new industrial order: carpets, curtains, fabrics, china, objets d'art, kitchen ranges, pots and pans. Such a household required higher standards of clearning, washing and laundering, and more complex cooking, reflecting the status of the home. The ready availability of domestic service meant that there was no need to save labour or limit acquisitions.

Women's labour was of course changed by the new urban environment in which they lived, though changes in patterns of housework were not necessarily immediate or dramatic. The tasks of fetching water and fuel, of cleaning, cooking and washing were not immediately transformed. Obtaining and transporting water was a routine everyday burden for working-class women until the late nineteenth century, a chore, almost always performed by women, not always recognized from a twentieth-century viewpoint. In the countryside, rainwater and private and public wells were used, though public wells could be at a considerable distance from housing. Water was carried in pitchers, tubs or buckets, sometimes on women's heads. In the towns there was likely to be some form of organized supply, mainly to pumps and to the houses of the wealthy. The problem was often that supplies could be intermittent and long waits for water could be necessary, with queues forming. In 1844 one engineer to the Southwark Water company in London reported 'I have seen as many as from 20 to 50 persons with pails waiting round one or two stand-pipes' (quoted in Davidson, 1982, p. 12). Fetching water could be a task which brought the women together – a place to stand and gossip – rather than being a private or domestic job.

Women's work was, then, dependent on changes in the organization of water supplies which had little to do with ideas about domesticity. There were important technical improvements from the late eighteenth century, but the most important though gradual changes followed the concern over public health in the 1830s and 1840s. From the middle of the nineteenth century local authorities began to take over water supplies, though supplying water to individual houses took a very long time. In Manchester a heavy investment in improving the water supplies was to mean internal water supplies in 80 percent of the city's 70,000 houses by 1876; but in many areas this took far longer. In the same period in London, working-class families were more likely to share outside taps. In the country, especially, labourers' houses with internal water supplies were still exceptional by the end of the century.

Laundry was an important part of the housework, and was

always women's work, whether performed by the housewife, by living-in domestic servants or by washerwomen. In the more remote areas of Britain, it might still be done close to a source of water – a river or well – and the clothes pounded or trampled till clean. Some kind of bleaching or cleansing agent which contained ammonia might be used – urine was apparently employed for this purpose. The most common cleansing solution used before soap was known as lye, which was water impregnated with alkaline salts from wood ashes; it was made by pouring the water through a frame like a sieve containing ashes. Soap was of course a great improvement on all these techniques, but was expensive and subject to excise duties: production, however, was expanding from the late seventeenth century, and was transformed by new methods of producing alkali from 1814 onwards. Nevertheless, until the mid-nineteenth century most households continued to use older methods, as well as soap if it could be afforded.

In prosperous homes washing would be done in a large copper, set in bricks with a fire underneath, built for the purpose. But in the first half of the century few poorer homes possessed such coppers, though they might be shared. Women might use the largest utensils they had, sometimes over a fire in the open air, and were likely to do the washing on the same day, Monday or Tuesday, sometimes sharing the labour. The importance of this labour was recognized by the inclusion of washhouses, shared between terraces or groups of houses, in new urban building for the poor. However the work was done, throughout this period it was a heavy and physically demanding task, with few technological improvements beyond the introduction of soap.

The open fire was at the begining of this period the universal source of warmth and of cooked food; but gradually women's housework was affected by changes in the fuel used, and in the technology of cooking, though only the better-off were likely to take full advantage of these. The rural poor used a variety of fuels for their fires – wood, peat, dung, gorse, seaweed – all of which had to be collected by members of the family. Not till after 1840, when railways brought down the costs of transport, did coal become the dominant fuel. Cooking in the late eighteenth century was dependent on the open fire: the most important technique for all classes was the boiling of food, in an open pot suspended over the fire. In this way the simplest meals such as boiled potatoes, porridge, stews, puddings and meat were cooked. This remained the recourse of the poor throughout the nineteenth century. Prosperous houses might also have a spit in front of the fire by which meat could be grilled, with various complex attachments for the regular turning of meat. Baking was, of course, also important and was normally done in the bread oven, usually of brick or stone, built over a fire and requiring ample fuel. Well-to-do houses might have their own separate ovens; but the poor were more likely to make use of a shared communal oven or use that of a baker. By the late eighteenth century the subject of cookery had already attracted a number of writers, both women and men, who saw it as a complex and challenging art, a part of rising domestic standards. But for the majority of women, cooking was a simple matter, dependent on sometimes scanty fuel, with food taking most of the family's monetary income. If resources were limited, then the communal oven might be used for the Sunday lunch.

The important change that did affect this process in the course of the nineteenth century was the introduction of the cast-iron range — first open, then closed — the product of the dramatically growing iron industry. The 'open' range saw the transition from an open fire to a narrowed grate, often adjustable in size, and often with a side boiler for heating water or an oven. The range was 'closed' when the open fire was completely covered on top by a hot plate and in front by a door. It was on sale commercially from the 1810s. Ovens and boilers could be built in on either side, and the closed range could became an elaborate affair designed to appeal to the better-off. The 'Kitchener' shown at the exhibition of 1851 was 18 ft long! The range was adopted only slowly into working-class homes: even in the 1890s many families would still depend on the open fire and use of the baker's oven. Gas made slow progress as a cooking fuel, and was first used in middle-class homes for cooking in the 1870s and 1880s; while coal remained cheap, it was the preferred fuel.

Cleaning, equally, was an almost universally female task; but there were virtually no changes in cleaning methods, with mops, brooms and brushes widely used. Soap or soda could not be widely used until the early nineteenth century: sand was often the preferred cleaning agent, but other minerals might be used. The cleaning of surfaces might involve decorative techniques, as with the whitening of hearthstones. Only with the coming of piped water and cheaper alkalis did technical changes affect cleaning, but this does not mean that practice was not altering. One historian of housework has written that 'between about 1670 and 1820 the status of cleaning was transformed; it ceased to be a peripheral aspect of housework and became one of central importance' (Davidson, 1982, p.128). There were a number of reasons for this. One was the spread of bedbugs, by the eighteenth century a menace to be constantly combated in the houses of the middle classes as in the poorer districts and the slums. And the more general use of coal in the urban environment meant constant smoke, grime and pollution. Increasing living standards for all classes by the end of the period brought with them new goods to be cleaned: wooden floors rather than earthen, linoleum and carpets, curtains and soft furnishings. The task of 'washing up' became a recognizable domestic duty only as mass produced crockery became increasingly more affordable. The new iron grates and ranges all needed regular blackleading to remain acceptable.

The young domestic servant entering a well-to-do household might well be bewildered by the luxury and the associated standards of cleanliness expected of her. But cleanliness, good housewifery and the management of a budget were important indicators of respectability for all. The servant's own horizons, once married with a home of her own, were likely to be limited by the family income: then, on the wages of a labourer or journeyman, the patterns of middle-class consumption would seem very distant. Yet the working-class woman would strive to demonstrate in constant battles against the pollution, dirt and bugs of urban life, in the whitening of the doorstep and the blackleading of the grate, the standards of her family to the rest of the neighbourhood.

By the end of this period, domestic labour had become, for some, a science: domestic science could be studied, and was taught in some elementary schools. It was argued that the care of the home was to be the future concern of working-class girls and its importance should be recognized. Yet the gap between the domestic experience of such teachers and the limited resources of the homes of such pupils still seems to have been unbridgeable. The limited resources of working-class households, and often the community basis of domestic life, influenced daughters more than the teaching they received at school. However, for a minority who had achieved higher incomes by the end of this period, the wives of artisans, engineers and foremen, the creation and maintaining of a domestic and private world could seem a route to a better future. Domestic aspirations were beginning to change in complex ways: working-class women too were influenced by the possibility of improved standards of living and tempted by the availability of new goods. They fought to achieve greater status through respectability, and watched the technological changes which by the late nineteenth century made piped water and iron ranges a reality for many.

### MOTHERHOOD

This issue is one of the most difficult which faces the historian of women's lives: it remains one about which we still know little. Some historians – notably Professor Lawrence Stone – have argued for a very significant change in the relationship between mothers and their infant children in the eighteenth century. They have suggested that high infant mortality rates and the harshness of living conditions characteristic of medieval and much of early modern society in England and Western Europe meant family relationships which were not strongly emotional: that in such societies the emotional ties between mothers and their children were not close, and that children were viewed by their parents in terms of the advantages they might bring or the burdens they might represent. This interpretation contrasts such a world with the increasingly affectionate family bonds to be found in certain social circles – the gentry, the urban middle classes – by the mid-eighteenth century. There, it was argued, the greater recognition of the distinct nature of childhood, and more stress on a mother's role in childrearing, was beginning to point the way to a family life more recognizable from the twentieth century.

There have been many critics of this kind of interpretation. It has been pointed out that these arguments rest on qualitative studies of very small and literate sections of the population, and that very little serious evidence has been produced for the family life of the majority. Linda Pollock suggests that a systematic study of diaries and autobiographies dealing with childhood from the seventeenth to the nineteenth centuries even among these literate groups suggests no great divergence of feeling. Parents in earlier societies also watched their children play, suffered great anxieties in their illnesses and grieved over their deaths. It is also misleading to draw too many conclusions from patterns of infant mortality. It is important to note that the high infant mortality rate – the rate of death of infants under one year – did not fall until the beginning of the twentieth century.

At present there is little detailed research to support arguments made either for a fundamental transformation of the quality of family life, or for a basic continuity with the world of the seventeenth century. We can hope only to indicate some of the questions which historians have been asking about the relationships between mothers and their children in this period.

The history of childbirth itself is beginning to be written, first by using the evidence of the medical profession, and then, very much more recently, through the writings of literate women. Linked to this must be the increasing role which the medical profession played in the nineteenth century in advising mothers on the care of children. Middle-class mothers were expected to bear a large part of the responsibility for the health and moral welfare of their children, especially for daughters, though their practical responsibilities for childcare might vary greatly depending on their wealth and numbers of servants. Working-class mothers might be blamed, as they were by many observers, for the inadequacies of their care: their children's diet, clothes and education might all be found lacking. The blame would be doubled when mothers worked in paid emploment outside the home. Changing roles within the family, sketched in chapters 2 and 3, meant that married women, housewives and mothers, carried a particular burden, that of the physical and emotional care of their families. Educational changes prolonged the period of childhood, as the family ceased to be the place where children were trained for their future. The exception to this lay in the training of girls; for mothers did prepare their daughters for their domestic destinies.

By the eighteenth century childbirth was being claimed as the province of the medical profession, and the right of the midwife to oversee childbirth was challenged. It is not easy to weigh up the consequences of this. It has been argued that the intervention of a financially interested, masculine profession, claiming a scientific authority unwarranted in the existing state of knowledge, imposed greater suffering on women, and helped to destroy the livelihood of the independent midwife. Certainly in early modern England there does appear to have been a female ritual of childbirth, with the husband excluded, when local women friends gathered together with the midwife to support the woman in labour, in a darkened room with spicy ale available. Doctors campaigned against this in the eighteenth century. And upper- and middle-class women, whenever possible, were attracted by the technical innovations and greater knowledge that a man-midwife, as they were at first called, seemed to offer. If they could afford the fees, such women were by the early nineteenth century increasingly likely to be attended by a doctor even for a normal birth. And we know that in aristocratic circles it was common for a husband to be present at the birth of a child. In the hospitals and growing medical schools of nineteenth-century England, obstetrics came very slowly to be recognized as a significant branch of medicine.

However, the extent of change for the majority of women can be exaggerated. The most obvious benefits for those who could afford medical care included the kind of wide-ranging obstetric knowledge, combined with a sensible reluctance to intervene, found in the most experienced practitioners of all. More obviously the use of chloroform from 1847 brought relief from pain to many. Yet the dangers of male medical management, compared to that of the midwife, have been related too. Overzealous intervention, including the use of forceps by many less experienced practitioners, could endanger the birth. Busy doctors in lying-in hospitals were a major source of puerperal infection. And some midwives had in the course of lengthy practice acquired an experience respected by leading doctors. Maternal mortality rates probably fell from estimated figures of just under 8 per 1,000 in the late eighteenth century to between 5 and 6 in the early nineteenth century, and then to 4 to 5 per 1,000 births, a figure which remained remarkably constant from 1847 to 1934. Medical changes, together with a more general fall in mortality rates, probably helped in the earlier reduction, but have to be set against the increasing risks of infection. Though frequent childbirth could be a source of chronic ill-health among women, it was not a major cause of death in women of childbearing age.

The midwife did not disappear in this period, but was likely still to attend the majority of births. The poor woman, unable to afford a medical presence, would rely on the service of a midwife, certainly for any normal birth at home. The demand for midwives remained, although they received no official recognition as a unique branch of the nursing profession until 1902.

Infant mortality rates, as has been suggested, remained high throughout this period, but the differences between region and class were subject to much contemporary study as they were recognized from the 1830s. There were striking disparities between urban and rural districts, and within urban areas between middle-class and working-class areas. So, in the 1850s the national average of infant mortality was 150 per 1,000 births, yet 94 per 1,000 in the 'healthiest' districts and

187 in the seven major towns of Yorkshire. In Bradford 20 per cent of infants − 200 out of every 1,000 − failed to live to twelve months.

Contemporary observers began to examine the reasons for these disparities. The main causes of death appeared to be different kinds of gastro-intestinal disorders, with symptoms of diarrhoea and dysentery. They looked at the appalling sanitary conditions and absence of water in crowded city conditions. And they looked particularly at the extent to which maternal negligence might be held responsible. They noted the apparent equation between areas of high female employment and those of high infant mortality. The obvious correlation seemed to be supported by the experience of the Lancashire cotton famine of 1862−4, when the American Civil War suspended supplies of cotton. Though there was high unemployment and consequent poverty, there was also a measurable drop in infant mortality. Later studies confirmed that the work of married women in industrial districts could be one factor affecting infant mortality, but that the most important was likely to be the general quality − and especially the sanitation − of the urban environment. As we have seen, a far smaller proportion of married women with young children were engaged in full-time work than many commentators imagined. Those who did work were likely to be those with low family incomes or few resources other than their own labours. Mothers worked from necessity to maintain support for their families.

The problem − which existed for women of all classes − was how to feed their infants in an age when medical opinion was coming to stress most strongly that there were no safe alternatives to breast feeding. For women for whom this was difficult, or who were working or away from home, there were few possibilities. Any kind of baby-minding was likely to involve artificial feeding of some kind. For the poor the milk available was dirty and adulterated: more common was a kind of bread and water 'pap'. 'Babies'' milk − a better quality of cow's milk sold in towns − was too expensive, as were feeding bottles and the prepared baby foods beginning to appear from the 1860s. A grandmother, neighbour or elder sister caring for an infant was most likely to offer milk and pap, perhaps sweetened by a little sugar or treacle, and to use some form of opiate to quiet a crying child. Overall, and away from the textile districts, most mothers were likely to feed their babies, often into their second year. Even so, in the larger towns, infant mortality remained high.

Well-to-do families at the beginning of the nineteenth century might still employ a wet nurse. Where in the eighteenth century children might have been sent away to nurse, increasingly the wet nurse was most likely to live in and be closely supervised. The wet nurse was therefore most likely to be young, single or widowed, having recently herself borne a child: needing income she would find the conditions of work likely to be good. The consequences were, however, only too often that the nurse's child, deprived of the mother's food, could be sacrificed. Partly for such reasons, opinion turned against the employment of wet nurses in the mid to late nineteenth century. In the 1860s and 1870s the *British Medical Journal* campaigned against both baby farming and wet nursing. In more modest middle-class families it is likely that breast feeding was most common throughout the century. In middle-class families, however, the new preparations, and feeding bottles with rubber teats, might be used from mid-century.

There were great contrasts between the experiences of mothers at different income levels. For the working-class woman of the early nineteenth century, caring for and supporting children had to be absorbed into the overwhelming necessity of maintaining the family income, whether this could best be achieved by her own casual labour, her domestic industry or her work for husband and children. Family life was lived at close quarters, with parents and four or five children within the tiny cottage or rooms that were home. To make this possible, order and obedience could be required and exacted. Children too had their obligations to work as best suited family needs: to assist at the loom, to mind the baby, to scare crows for the farmer. This is not to suggest that childhood did not exist: working-class parents recognized the need for education and set aside small sums to send their children to whatever small schools existed, but sooner rather than later a family's need for a child's income would prevail. There was a degree of over-lapping of tasks between girls and boys, but mothers were likely to see their daughters as contributing both to the family economy and to their own labours. Some mothers were likely to be able to train daughters at home, to finish lace or sew on buttons; others might see their daughters enter the local mill, working long hours, bringing home money, but unable to offer domestic help; others again might send daughters at twelve or thirteen into service in some middle-class household, to appear again at home only briefly on scarce days off.

In the course of the nineteenth century there were important shifts in this relationship. School was a major part of the childhood of the great majority of girls and boys by the 1880s where it had not been in the 1830s; and the schooling received was likely to reinforce the importance attached to order and discipline within the home. It was likely also to reinforce the expectations of young girls, already acquired at home, that their future destiny was to lie in the domestic world. Daughters were likely to be called upon to perform a range of domestic tasks by their mothers which might provide a kind of training for their future life. Such a training would be much more significant to them than the lessons in needlework and cooking which were increasingly to be a part of elementary-school curricula for girls, lessons which often seemed remote and irrelevant.

For working-class mothers and children, childhood itself could be brief. Even the coming of compulsory education provided only for its lasting to the age of twelve. The age of consent too remained at twelve until 1886. There was a gulf between the expectations of middle-class and working-class parents. The difference reflected the harshness of the environ-ment in which working-class girls and boys had to be equipped to find their way and make their livings. A mother had to use their resources in the family interest and also to help prepare them for an adult life in that world. Yet that did not imply an uncaring relationship, or that mothers did not grieve as they experienced the illness and death of infants and children, as they too frequently might do.

The responsibilities of middle-class parents could last much longer. Daughters were likely to remain in the parental home with their mothers until marriage. Sons might require secondary and higher education and further professional training. Mothers from the well-to-do middle classes were likely to employ nurses and nannies for the physical care of their children: the nursery could become the focus of their lives, remote from the world of their parents. For some children in this situation, their mother could seem a distant and occasional presence, but for others the few hours a day spent with her were likely to be affectionate and close.

In more modest middle-class families no such barriers could exist, and there a mother's work was likely to be demanding. Among such families the central importance of women's task as mothers was likely to be stressed. The wealth of prescriptive literature addressed to such social groups suggests to what extent mothers were seen as responsible not only for the physical well-being but for the moral character and future of their children. Their oversight of early education, of moral and spiritual training, and their daily responsibility for the good health of their young, emerges from any detailed study of their worlds. We know that some mothers, like Elizabeth Gaskell, kept detailed daily records of their children's progress, both educational and spiritual, from an early age, writing also of the death of a much-loved child. In such families there was time and leisure for children to play, as nurses and mothers might encourage appropriate activities for girls and boys. Boys were unlikely to be taught at home after the age of six to seven; mothers remained in charge of the care of daughters, even if a governess was employed or daughters sent to local schools. Daughters might be sent for a time to academies, or, later in the period, to secondary schools, but they were most likely to return home and lead a domestic and sociable life, regulated by their mothers, and guided by their parents in the choice of partner.

Motherhood was clearly idealized or sentimentalized in much of the literature addressed to such moderately prosperous families. The responsibilities of motherhood were stressed equally by medical men and by legislators. Working-class mothers were as likely to follow the commonly received standards of the new urban communities, of neighbouring families and friends. Being a good and responsible mother could be an element in achieving respectable status: even those who did not aim so high had as their priority keeping the family economy afloat, by whatever strategies came to hand.


DOMESTIC SERVICE

The domestic servant was both a paid employee and a member of a household, and by the late nineteenth century the experience of being a domestic servant was a very common one. It may seem strange that in an industrialized society the most common form of employment for a young woman was to be a domestic servant; but the growth in demand for servants from the well-to-do and even the modestly well-off, and the absence of other kinds of employment for young women, meant that by the 1880s perhaps around a third of all young women between fifteen and twenty-one were likely to be in service.

These figures reflect the census returns, and as we have already seen, such figures can be misleading. They can be particularly misleading in the case of domestic servants. It is easy to assume that the characteristic experience was that of the young woman in the well-to-do household, sharing domestic work, and the social life of a servants' hall, with other servants. Many young women would still in country areas be farm servants, doing whatever was needed on the farm; in the town they might work in a shop or workshop, again at whatever was needed. The work that they did could not be easily labelled as domestic work. So in 1851 a confectioner of Heywood, Lazarus Collinge, employed a girl 'to learn his trade and perform domestic duties' (quoted in Higgs, 1986, p. 41). Similarly, not all those who employed servants were necessarily prosperous. In a study of those who kept servants in Rochdale, some 16 per cent of householders with living-in servants were artisans, clerks or manual workers. The majority of such servants were likely to be general servants, doing everything necessary for the household.

There is also the difficult question of who became servants. Another way in which the census returns are inaccurate is that they tend to record as 'servants' (which we would interpret as those paid for their services) family members. So widows who were the heads of their household might be recorded as 'housekeepers', and daughters as 'servants'. In one Rochdale case in 1851 the Bollitt family included John Bollitt, a hair-dresser, his wife Ann and three children under ten; it also included Sally Howarth, Ann's sister, described as a 'general servant' (quoted in Higgs, 1986, p. 125). Clearly someone was needed at home whether to run the shop or care for the children.

More generally, domestic service was related to the local employment situation for young women. Not all middle-class families kept servants, especially if there were a number of female relatives or daughters in the same house. If there were alternative kinds of employment easily available, then it might prove difficult for middle-class employers to find a live-in servant. In some northern textile cities, servants were a much smaller proportion of the female workforce, and non-resident servants, living at home and coming to work daily, were more common. But in the older cities and small towns, service could be the major source of employment. In the countryside also, especially in areas where farm service was less common, young girls were likely to leave their homes at the age of twelve or thirteen to enter service. With the decline of agricultural work for women, such girls were likely to find it hard to stay in their rural homes.

Domestic service was not only a means of employment: it could also be seen as a form of poor relief. Many young girls and women might enter service from workhouses and charitable institutions. Families in modest circumstances looking for a servant might well visit a local workhouse and select a girl, sometimes as young as ten or twelve. Such servants were lucky to receive any wages at all beyond their board. Charitable institutions too would encourage domestic service as the only way in which their girls could be placed to earn their keep. Philanthropists like Louisa Twining, investigating their situation in the 1860s, found former workhouse girls paid around a pound a year besides their board. And some women regarded as 'fallen women' by society — because they had been prostitutes or convicted criminals — might be encouraged to redeem themselves at first in refuges or Magdalen Homes, and then in some kind of domestic service.

Domestic service, then, might take many forms. For the young woman it was likely, in most areas of the country, to be a significant possibility, a stage through which many would pass. Few were likely to regard it as an occupation for life. It was clearly an occupation, which for most brought no common feeling with other servants. A small minority, who worked in the large establishments of the aristocracy and gentry, might experience the world of the servants' hall with its own hierarchy and career structure of male and female servants, running from the well-paid housekeeper, to lady's maid, cook, parlour maid, and at the other extreme the lowly scullery maid. Some would be relatively well paid, though they were also likely to work very long hours. But the majority would find themselves in smaller households, probably doing all the major domestic work for a middle-class or lower-middle-class family. In doing so, such servants would have to adapt to their family's notions of propriety, cleanliness and an ordered way of life. The domestic servant was of course expected to know her place within the household, and that place was a lowly one. Servants' time was at the disposal of their employer; little free time was likely to be given. Deference and obedience were expected from the servant, though there were of course ways in which servants might try to maintain their own positions. One way was to change jobs: there was a high level of mobility among domestic servants.

We still have to reflect upon the consequences of this experience of domestic service for so many women. It has been argued that service was one major route by which the ideals of domesticity were adopted by working-class households. It may be that in setting up their own homes, former servants did recollect the ways of keeping house which they had learned. But their own aspirations were always likely to be restrained by their housing and their incomes. The young woman from a country background who returned home to marry a labourer was unlikely to be able to afford to look back to the life of her middle-class employer. But the better-off servants might well, through contacts made in service, be likely to court and marry the tradesmen, shopkeepers and skilled craftsmen of the lower middle classes, with a commitment to maintaining a level of respectability.

Marriage was likely to end recorded employment as a domestic servant: but domestic labour, though it was rarely formally recorded, remained one of the most important and continuing areas of labour for the working-class married woman in the nineteenth century. One way in which a married woman or a widow might earn money would be to take in lodgers and provide services for them. So a woman with a spare room might charge a basic rental and earn more by doing a lodger's washing and providing meals. This might be a particularly useful resource for ex-domestic servants; it might also be important for those with very young children, or those whose children had left home. But to do this it was necessary to have sufficient space.

For the older woman, washing, charring, mangling and ironing were all possible ways to increase the family income: this could be very hard physical work, performed either in someone else's house or in one's own home. It was likely to be casual and irregular. It might be performed in areas of high female employment for younger women workers, where childminders, teamakers and washerwomen might be in demand. It might − like washing and mangling − be performed for another woman running a small laundering business. Or it could simply be undertaken as casual employment, performed for better-off middle-class families. We know from surveys made of the condition of working-class families at the end of the nineteenth century by Charles Booth and by Seebohm Rowntree just how common this kind of work was and how critical to the subsistence of the poorest families (Meacham, 1977, pp. 99−100).

Residential domestic service may have reached its height in the 1860s and 1870s. It is clear that where alternative kinds of employment existed for young women, then they would take

101

those jobs: young women disliked the restraints and the obedience expected in domestic service. Employers clearly preferred girls from the country to urban young women, who might be more aware of alternative possibilities, more independent in their lifestyle. As more and more productive activities, and services, came to be concentrated outside the home, so young women chose different kinds of jobs, in factories, as shop assistants or clerks. Yet, although by the late nineteenth century domestic service was no longer expanding so rapidly, domestic labour remained a particularly important area of women's work, and one which was not always easy to disentangle from unpaid work performed for one's family. As we have seen, the boundaries between the world of the family and those of work could not be clearly drawn, even at the end of our period. In Victorian society, domestic labour most clearly illustrates how the division of labour within the family extended into the world of paid employment.

# References and Further Reading

The following is a very selective bibliography, based on references in this work. The place of publication is London unless otherwise stated.

Alexander, Sally 1976: Women's work in nineteenth century London 1820–1850. In Juliet Mitchell and Ann Oakley (eds), *The Rights and Wrongs of Women*, Penguin.

Anderson, Michael 1971a: Family, household and the industrial revolution. In M. Anderson (ed.), *Sociology of the Family*, Penguin.

Anderson, Michael 1971b: *Family Structure in Nineteenth Century Lancashire*. Cambridge: Cambridge University Press.

Anderson, Michael 1980: *Approaches to the History of the Western Family, 1500–1914*. Macmillan.

Berg, M. 1985: *The Age of Manufactures: Industry, Innovation and Work in Britain 1700–1820*. Fontana.

Berg, M. 1987: Women's work, mechanisation and the early phases of industrialisation in England. In P. Joyce (ed.), *The Historical Meanings of Work*, Cambridge: Cambridge University Press.

Blackstone, W. 1771: *Commentaries on the Laws of England*. 4th edn, 4 vols, Dublin.

Bornat, Joanna 1985: Lost leaders: women, trade unionism and the case of the general union of textile workers, 1875–1914. In Angela John (ed.), *Unequal Opportunities*.

Branca, Patricia 1975: *Silent Sisterhood: Middle Class Women in the Victorian Home*. Croom Helm.

Burnett, John 1978: *A Social History of Housing 1815–1970*. Newton Abbot: David & Charles.

Bythell, Duncan 1969: *The Handloom Weavers: A Study in the English Cotton Industry during the Industrial Revolution.* Cambridge: Cambridge University Press.

Bythell, Duncan 1978: *The Sweated Trades: Outwork in Nineteenth Century Britain.* Batsford.

Davidoff, Leonore 1979: The separation of home and work? Landladies and lodgers in nineteenth and twentieth century England. In Sandra Burman (ed.), *Fit Work for Women*, London and Canberra: Croom Helm.

Davidoff, Leonore and Hall, Catherine 1987: *Family Fortunes: Men and Women of the English Middle Classes 1780–1850.* Hutchinson.

Davidoff, Leonore, Newby, Howard and L'Esperance, Jean 1976: Landscape without figures: home and community in English society. In Juliet Mitchell and Ann Oakley (eds), *The Rights and Wrongs of Women*, Penguin.

Davidson, Caroline 1982: *'A Woman's Work is Never Done': A History of Housework in the British Isles 1650–1950.* Chatto and Windus.

Donnison, Jean 1977: *Midwives and Medical Men: A History of Inter-Professional Rivalries and Women's Rights.* Heinemann.

Dyhouse, Carol 1981: *Girls Growing Up in Late Victorian and Edwardian England.* Routledge and Kegan Paul.

Faderman, Lilian 1981: *Surpassing the Love of Men: Romantic Friendship and Love between Women from the Renaissance to the Present.* Women's Press.

Fox, Eliza 1869: *Memoir.* Ed. Franklin Fox.

Gillis, J. 1983: Servants, sexual relations and the risks of illegitimacy in London, 1801–1900. In Judith Newton et al. (eds), *Sex, Class and Politics*, Routledge and Kegan Paul.

Gillis, J. R. 1985: *For Better, For Worse: British Marriages 1600 to the Present.* New York: Oxford University Press.

Hakim, Catherine 1980: Census reports as documentary evidence: the census commentaries 1801–1951. *Sociological Review*, 28, 551–79.

Hall, Catherine 1979: The early formation of Victorian domestic ideology. In Sandra Burman (ed.), *Fit Work for Women*, Croom Helm.

Hellerstein, Erna A., Hume, Lesley P. and Offen, Karen M. (eds) 1981: *Victorian Women: A Documentary Account of Women's Lives in Nineteenth Century France, England, and America.* Harvester Press.

Henriques, U. R. Q. 1967: Bastardy and the New Poor Law. *Past and Present*, 37, 103-29.

104

Hewitt, Margaret 1958: *Wives and Mothers in Victorian Industry*. Rockliff.

Higgs, Edward 1986: *Domestic Servants and Households in Rochdale 1851 to 1871*. New York: Garland.

Hill, Bridget 1983: *Eighteenth Century Women: An Anthology*. George Allen and Unwin.

Holcombe, Lee 1973: *Victorian Ladies at Work: Middle Class Working Women in England and Wales 1850–1914*. Newton Abbot: David & Charles.

Holcombe, Lee 1983: *Wives and Property: Reform of the Married Women's Property Law*. Oxford: Martin Robertson.

Horn, Pamela 1975: *The Rise and Fall of the Victorian Servant*. Dublin: Gill and Macmillan.

Horstman, Allen 1986: *Victorian Divorce*. Croom Helm.

Humphries, Jane 1981: Protective legislation, the capitalist state, and working class men: the case of the 1842 Mines Regulation Act. *Feminist Review*, 7, 1–33.

John, Angela 1980: *By the Sweat of their Brow: Women Workers at Victorian Coal Mines*. Routledge and Kegan Paul.

John, Angela (ed.) 1985: *Unequal Opportunities: Women's Employment in England 1800–1918*. Oxford: Basil Blackwell.

Kamm, Josephine 1965: *Hope Deferred: Girls' Education in English History*. Methuen.

Laqueur, T. W. 1974: Literacy and social mobility in the Industrial Revolution in England. *Past and Present*, 64, 96–107.

Lazonick, William 1979: Industrial relations and technical change: the case of the self-acting mule: *Cambridge Journal of Economics*, 3, 231–49.

Levine, David 1977: *Family Formation in an Age of Nascent Capitalism*. New York: Academic Press.

Levine, David 1985: Industrialization and the proletarian family in England. *Past and Present*, 107, 168–203.

Lewenhak, Sheila 1977: *Women and Trade Unions: An Outline History of Women in the British Trade Union Movement*. Ernest Benn.

Lewis, Judith Schneid 1986: *In the Family Way: Childbearing in the British Aristocracy 1760–1860*. New Brunswick, NJ: Rutgers University Press.

Lindert, T. H. 1980: English occupations, 1670–1811. *Journal of Economic History*, 40, 685–712.

Lown, Judy 1983: Not so much a factory, more a form of patriarchy: gender and class during industrialisation. In Eva Gamarnikow et al. (eds), *Gender, Class and Work*, Heinemann.

McBride, Theresa 1976: *The Domestic Revolution: The Modernisation of Household Service in England and France, 1820–1920*. Croom Helm.

Macfarlane, A. 1986: *Marriage and Love in England: Modes of Reproduction 1300–1840*. Oxford: Basil Blackwell.

Maclaren, Angus 1978: *Birth Control in Nineteenth Century England*. Croom Helm.

Maclaren, Angus 1984: *Reproductive Rituals: The Perception of Fertility in England from the Sixteenth Century to the Nineteenth Century*. Methuen.

Meacham, Standish 1977: *A Life Apart: The English Working Class 1890–1914*. Thames and Hudson.

Menefee, S. P. 1981: *Wives for Sale: An Ethnographic Study of British Popular Divorce*. Oxford: Basil Blackwell.

More, Hannah 1818: *Strictures on the Modern System of Female Education*. 1799, in *The Works of Hannah More*, London, vol. 8.

Murray, Janet Horowitz 1982: *Strong-Minded Women and Other Lost Voices from 19th Century England*. Penguin.

Osterud, Nancy Grey 1986: Gender divisions and the organization of work in the Leicester hosiery industry. In Angela John (ed.), *Unequal Opportunities*.

Pedersen, Joyce 1988: *The Reform of Girls' Secondary and Higher Education in Victorian England: A Study of Elites and Educational Change*. New York: Garland.

Peterson, M. J. 1972: The Victorian governess. In M. Vicinus (ed.), *Suffer and be Still*.

Pinchbeck, Ivy 1981: *Women Workers and the Industrial Revolution, 1750–1850*. 1930, rpt Virago.

Pollock, Linda 1983: *Forgotten Children: Parent-Child Relations from 1500 to 1900*. Cambridge: Cambridge University Press.

Porter, G. R. 1843: *The Progress of the Nation*. 3 vols.

Rendall, Jane 1985: *The Origins of Modern Feminism: Women in Britain, France, and the United States, 1780–1860*. Macmillan.

*Report of the Commissioners on the Employment of Women and Children in Agriculture* 1843: XII.

Richards, Eric 1974: Women in the British economy since about 1700: an interpretation. *History*, 59, 337–47.

Sanderson, M. 1983: *Education, economic change, and society in England 1780–1870*. Macmillan.

Snell, K. D. M. 1985a: Agricultural seasonal unemployment, the standard of living, and women's work in the south and east, 1690–1860. In *Annals of the Labouring Poor*, Cambridge: Cambridge University Press.

Snell, K. D. M. 1985b: The apprenticeship of women. In *Annals of the Labouring Poor*, Cambridge: Cambridge University Press.

Snell, K. D. M. 1985c: The family. In *Annals of the Labouring Poor*. Cambridge: Cambridge University Press.

Stanley, Liz (ed.) 1984: *The Diaries of Hannah Cullwick, Victorian Maidservant*. Virago.

Steedman, Carolyn 1982: *The Tidy House: Little Girls Writing*. Virago.

Stone, Lawrence 1977: *The Family, Sex and Marriage in England, 1500–1800*. Weidenfeld & Nicolson.

Summers, Anne 1983: Ladies and nurses in the Crimean War. *History Workshop Journal*, 16, 33–56.

Taylor, Barbara 1983: *Eve and the New Jerusalem: Socialism and Feminism in the Nineteenth Century*. Virago.

Thomis, Malcolm I. and Grimmett, Jennifer 1982: *Women in Protest, 1800–1850*. Croom Helm.

Thompson, E. P. 1972: 'Rough music': le charivari anglais. *Annales ESC*, 27, 285–312.

Thompson, E. P. and Yeo, E. (eds) 1971: *The Unknown Mayhew: Selections from the Morning Chronicle, 1849–50*. Penguin.

Tilly, Louise and Scott, Joan 1978: *Women, Work and Family*. New York: Holt, Rinehart and Winston.

Vicinus, Martha (ed.) 1972: *Suffer and be Still: Women in the Victorian Age*. Bloomington and London: Indiana University Press.

Vicinus, Martha 1977: *A Widening Sphere: Changing Roles of Victorian Women*. Bloomington and London: Indiana University Press.

Vicinus, Martha 1985: *Independent Women: Work and Community for Single Women, 1850–1920*. Virago.

Vincent, David 1981: *Bread, Knowledge and Freedom: A Study of Nineteenth Century Working Class Autobiography*. Cambridge: Cambridge University Press.

Whitbread, Helena (ed.) 1988: *'I Know My Own Heart': The Diaries of Anne Lister 1791–1840*. Virago.

Widdowson, Frances 1980: *Going Up into the Next Class: Women and Elementary Teacher Training*. Women's Research and Resources Centre.

Wilberforce, W. 1797: *A Practical View of the Prevailing Religious System of Professed Christians in the Higher and Middle Classes in this Country, contrasted with Real Christianity*. 2nd edn.

Wrigley, E. A., and Schofield, R. S. 1981: *The Population History of England 1541–1871*. Edward Arnold.

# Index

framework knitters, 23, 67, 83
  in Leicestershire, 9–10

gas
  introduction of, 88–9
  lighting, 82
Gaskell, Dr, 60
Gaskell, Elizabeth, 4, 60, 97
General Union of Textile
    Workers, 64
George IV, King, 48
Gilbert, Ann Taylor, 46, 47
Girls' Public Day School Trust,
    73
Girton College, 73
governesses, 72
Guest, John, 50
guilds, 28

Hamilton, Elizabeth, 47
Hardwicke's Act (1754), 34
heavy industry, expansion in, 57
Hitchinson, George, 42
Home and Colonial Infant
    School Society, 74
Home and Colonial Training
    College, 74
hosiery manufacture, 9–10, 19
*Household Management* (Beeton),
    5
'housewife', meaning of word, 85
housework, 85–90
housing, 8, 81–5
Humphries, Jane, 62
Hutton, William, 25

industrial revolution, 11, 12
industrialization, impact of,
    4–10

James, John Angell, 46
japanning/lacquering trade, 31

Kaiserwerth, 76
Kenrick, Samuel, 53
*Kirsteen* (Oliphant), 65
'Kitchener', 88

labour
  in agriculture, 15–16
  cheap, 12, 23, 32
  division of, 8–9, 25–6, 102
  (un)skilled, 5
lace making industry, 67
'Ladies of Llangollen', 49
Lady Margaret Hall College, 73
laundry, 86–7
law
  and factory work, 60–1
  and marriage, 34–5, 79–80
leisure, 3
lesbianism, 49
Lewis, Sarah, 2
Limited Liability Act (1856/7),
    52–3
Lister, Anne, 49
literacy, 73–4
London Society of Compositors,
    The, 65
Long, Jane, 17
Loudon, John Claudius, 81
Lown, Judy, 59, 63

Magdalen Homes, 100
male/female, clear separation of,
    46–7
Manners, Lord, 9, 62
*Manual of Domestic Economy*
    (Walsh), 81
*Manufacturing Population of
    England, The* (Dr Gaskell),
    60
marriage, 8, 15, 53–4, 101
  age of participants, 37
  formal structure, 34–5

*Index by Geraldine Beare*